NIGERIA:

A COMPLEX NATION AT A CROSSROADS IN AFRICA AND THE WORLD

Does the World need Nigeria?

"It is critical to the rest of the continent, and if Nigeria does not get it right, Africa will really not make more progress".

—American President Barack Obama

Yemi Adesina

ISBN: 000-0-00000-000-0

CONTENTS

Acknowledgements

Although one man has written this book, it wouldn't have been possible without the many people who have been so inspirational and whose research and hard work were helpful during its writing.

I am thankful to God Almighty for His grace to research and put my findings into a book.

I also owe much to the many people who have encouraged me to follow my dream. In particular, my late dad, Mr Solomon Olajide Adesina. And to Bola, my wife of 27 years of marriage. I thank her immensely for her undying love, support, and encouragement, which allowed me to travel, research, and practise farming in Africa for many years.

For my two sons, Femi and Seun, whose input as the second-generation African diaspora in the United Kingdom makes the book more relevant to younger Africans. I want to thank them for our lengthy chats and the healthy debates that lasted late into the night and early mornings to gather their perspectives on specific topics. I firmly believe their generation and those following beyond will move Africa further into the future.

Many people influenced me to start learning about Africa. Some of them I have met in person, and some I know through their teachings, lectures, training, research books and journals. Coming from all walks of life, the variety of sources, expertise and professions assisted me in approaching the issue from different perspectives, adding much value to this book.

My inspirations were Pastor Matthew Ashimolowo, the late Dr Myles Munro, Dr Mensah Otabil, and Bishop Tudor Bismark. These pastors spent a lot of time teaching and believing Africa could improve.

I am greatly indebted to Dr Toyin Falola, an African historian, Dr Howard Nicholas, an economist and researcher at Erasmus University Rotterdam, and Jeffrey D. Sachs et al. for their input on the impact of geography. I am further indebted to Quoras.com, Walter Rodney *for How Europe Underdeveloped Africa.* Finally, I thank Yemi Adeyemi, the founder of ThinkAfrica.net.

Foreword

Nigeria is a country of great significance in Africa and the world. Nigeria is the heartbeat of Africa! With a population of over 200 million people, it is the most populous country in Africa and the seventh most populous country in the world. Nigeria has much to offer to the world, from its strategic location, rich natural resources, and cultural diversity to its vibrant business scene.

Located in West Africa, Nigeria is strategically positioned as a gateway to the rest of the continent. It shares borders with Benin, Niger, Chad, and Cameroon and has access to the Gulf of Guinea, making it a major maritime hub. Nigeria's location also gives it significant regional political and economic influence.

Nigeria is the largest economy in Africa and one of the fastest-growing in the world. With a rapidly expanding middle class and a young and ambitious workforce, the opportunities for growth and innovation are endless, and the future is bright for Nigeria. The country's oil and gas, telecommunications, and banking sectors are driving economic growth and providing opportunities for investment and development.

But it's not just about business. Nigeria is a melting pot of cultures, languages, and traditions, home to over 500 ethnic groups with unique cultures, traditions, and languages. The country's diversity has contributed to its vibrant music, literature, and art scenes, making it a cultural hub in Africa and worldwide. Nigeria is a land of contrasts and possibilities, from bustling cities to the lush countryside. Nigeria's cultural heritage is also reflected in its religious diversity, with Christianity, Islam, and traditional religions practised widely.

Nigeria's economic and political influence extends beyond its borders, with more than 20 million Nigerians in the diaspora paying an estimated $25 billion in annual remittances. Nigerians are among the highest educated migrants and the most successful ethnic group in the United States. They have distinguished themselves as highly-educated achievers in music, medicine, business and corporate enterprise, sports, music, education, and other sectors of the diaspora economy.

Nigeria plays a significant role in the global economy as the largest economy in Africa and a member of the United Nations (UN) and the G20 group of nations. As the largest economy in Africa, it represents the continent's interests within the G20. Through its participation in the G20, Nigeria has been able to voice the concerns of African countries and promote the importance of addressing issues such as poverty, inequality, and sustainable development. Nigeria also plays a key role in regional organizations such as the Economic Community of West African States (ECOWAS) and the African Union (AU).

Arguably, no country is indispensable. While other countries on the continent of Africa can and may survive without Nigeria, any emerging country on the continent would be foolish to ignore or not tap into the market of 200 million people in Nigeria.

Nigeria's importance in Africa and the world cannot be overstated. Understanding Nigeria's history, politics, economy, society, and culture is essential to understanding its role in the world and its prospects for the future. So, does the world need Nigeria? The answer is a resounding yes.

The Author

Mr Yemi Adesina is the founder of Boyd Agro-Allied Ltd, one of the largest pig farms in Nigeria. He is also the CEO of Pristine Integrated Farm Resources Ltd, a non-profit organisation registered in Africa to promote youth and rural empowerment, alleviate poverty in Africa through education, and improve the productivity and livelihood of farmers from subsistence to commercial farming in Africa.

He is a social worker, a seasoned farmer and a prolific trainer. He posted 150 videos on YouTube (papayemo1) covering the different aspects of pig farming and African History. Over 2.5 million viewers watched the videos in over 36 countries, making it one of the most-watched videos on YouTube from an African perspective.

He is the author of "*Why Africa Cannot Feed Itself and the Way Forward*", "*Profitable Pig Farming: A Step-by-Step Guide to Commercial Pig Farming from an African Perspective*", "*What the Ancient African Knew*" and "*Does the World Need Africa*".

Mr Yemi, a diaspora, emigrated to the United Kingdom in 1991. He studied and worked for 20 years and earned his Master's in Business Administration and Master's in Social Work in the United Kingdom. In 2010, he emigrated to Nigeria to contribute to Nigeria's food production.

Purpose and Scope of the Book

The primary objective of this book is to provide an in-depth analysis of Nigeria's history, politics, economy, culture, and society. The book aims to offer readers a comprehensive understanding of Nigeria as a country, its place in Africa, how its citizenry is perceived worldwide, and the challenges and opportunities it faces as it seeks to realize its potential.

The book will cover a range of themes, including Nigeria's pre-colonial and colonial history, its struggle for independence, the impact of military rule, the transition to democracy, economic development, social and cultural diversity, and Nigeria's role in regional and international affairs. Each chapter will focus on a specific theme, providing a detailed analysis and highlighting key issues and debates.

The book is aimed at a general audience, including young people, students, scholars, policymakers, journalists, and anyone interested in Africa and Nigeria's history, politics, and society. The book is designed to provide readers with a comprehensive and accessible overview of Nigeria and its significance while offering insights into the country's challenges and opportunities.

The book will take a multidisciplinary approach, drawing on insights and perspectives from history, political science, economics, sociology, anthropology, and other disciplines. It will incorporate a range of primary and secondary sources, including academic literature, government reports, media sources, and interviews with experts and stakeholders.

1. Introduction

Nigeria, located in West Africa, is bordered in the north by Niger, east by Chad and Cameroon, south by the Gulf of Guinea of the Atlantic Ocean, and west by Benin. Nigeria is larger than the U.S. state of Texas. Its population is over 200 million people (about half of the United States), making it the most populous country in Africa and the seventh most populous country globally. The country is a melting pot of cultures and traditions. It has a diverse population, with over 500 ethnic groups and over 1000 languages spoken, and its people are known for their resilience and determination in facing challenges. The official language is English, but the most widely spoken languages are Hausa, Yoruba and Ibo.

Throughout its history, Nigeria has played a vital role in the continent and the world, from its rich cultural heritage to its economic power, political stability, and human capital. Nigeria is also known for its rich history and abundant natural resources. Nigerian music, film and literature are well-known across the globe, and the country is also home to a thriving fashion and art scene. But despite all of these assets, the question remains: "Does the world need Nigeria?

Whether the world needs Nigeria is a complex and fascinating topic that has been debated for decades. To explore this question excitingly and interestingly, we will delve into the rich history of Nigeria. We will closely examine Nigeria's current state of affairs and explore the strengths and weaknesses that have impacted its global standing, how Nigeria has contributed to the world and the key events and figures that have shaped the country.

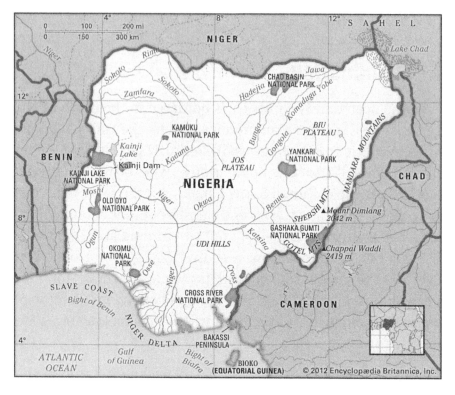

Map of Nigeria *https://www.britannica.com/*

We will begin by journeying through time, tracing the evolution of Nigeria from its earliest days to the present. From the pre-colonial era to the present day, we will explore the political, economic, and social developments that have shaped the country and examine the legacy of slavery and colonialism and the struggles for independence that defined Nigeria's early years as a nation. We will explore the impact of key historical figures, such as the great warrior Queen Amina, Madame Nwanyeruwa, and Funmilayo Anikulapo-Kuti. We will also examine the legendary anti-colonial leaders Tafawa Balewa,

Herbert Macaulay, Obafemi Awolowo, and Nnamdi Azikiwe and learn how their actions shaped the country's trajectory.

As we journey through the pages of this book, we will encounter a wide range of perspectives, from those who believe that Nigeria is an indispensable player on the world stage to those who argue that the country is a burden on the global community. We will consider the role of key industries, such as oil and agriculture, and how they have affected Nigeria's economy and global standing. We will also consider Nigeria's complex and often conflicting realities and discover why this African giant continues to be such a controversial and fascinating subject.

As we move into the present day, we will look closely at Nigeria's current political, economic, and social situation. We will examine the country's strengths and weaknesses and explore how they have impacted its global standing. We will also delve into Nigeria's challenges, such as poverty, corruption, and political instability. In recent years, Nigeria has also faced economic challenges, including the fall in oil prices, COVID 19 and the devaluation of the local currency. We will explore how these challenges have affected the country's ability to contribute to the world and the efforts made by its government and its people to address them.

But it's not all doom and gloom; Nigeria has also significantly contributed to the world. Nigeria has left its mark on the global stage and has contributed to the music and film industry as well as to science and technology. We will explore these contributions in-depth and discover why Nigeria is considered an important player on the world stage.

We will deliberate in detail on how other African countries and the world perceive Nigerians in the diaspora. Some Africans admire Nigerians for their outgoing, friendly and entrepreneurial spirit. At the same time, some perceive them as arrogant and overly ambitious, with a certain degree of suspicion and a tendency to dominate and intimidate others. We will also look at the perspectives of the people of Nigeria, their drives, aspirations and reality, the diversity of Nigerian society, and the role of ethnic and religious groups in shaping the country's identity—also, the Nigerian diaspora's role and impact on the country's image and economy. We will review the role of women and minorities in Nigeria, including their participation in politics, the economy and society from pre-colonial times till to date.

Furthermore, we will also examine the impact of Nigeria's burgeoning youth population on the country's future. Nigeria's Millennials and Generation Z population is one of the largest in the world aspirations, and potential roles are shaping the country's future.

Ultimately, we will draw together all the information gathered to conclude whether the world needs Nigeria. It's an exciting and thought-provoking journey that will give you a deeper understanding of this complex and fascinating country.

In summary, this book aims to learn about past events and understand how they have shaped the country's present and will continue to shape its future. This will help us better understand the country's role in the global community and how it can continue contributing to the world.

Winston Churchill says, "Those that fail to learn from history are doomed to repeat it." A quote from Machiavelli said, "Whoever wishes to foresee the future must consult the past; for human events ever resemble those of preceding times. This arises from the fact that they are produced by men who ever have been, and ever shall be, animated by the same passions, and thus they necessarily have the same results."

In conclusion, arguably, no country is indispensable. While other countries on the continent of Africa can and may survive without Nigeria, any emerging country on the continent would be foolish to ignore or not tap into the market of 200 million people in Nigeria. "Does the World Need Nigeria" — absolutely. Nigeria is an essential part of the global community and has the potential to make a significant impact in the world. It is up to the country, its people, and the international community to work together to support its growth and development so that Nigeria can continue to impact the world and reach its full positive potential.

2. Nigeria's Rich History Dates Back to Pre-Colonial Times

Nigeria has a rich history dating back to pre-colonial times. Archaeological evidence suggests that human habitation in the area now known as Nigeria dates back to at least 11,000 BC. The oldest fossils found by Nigerian archaeologists date back to 9000 BCE.

Humans produced hunting weapons and non-metals like ceramics and terracotta sculptures during this era. The earliest identifiable culture in Nigeria's history is the Nok culture. The Nok culture appeared in northeastern Nigeria around 1500 BC in Jos plateau state and was one of the earliest ironworking societies from western Africa. In the 1930s, the tin miners in Jos Plateau state accidentally discovered terracotta figurines that the Nok people produced. Since this discovery, Nok sculptures have been found across over 78,000 square kilometres (30,116 square miles), suggesting these artists were part of an expansive civilisation. The area was later settled by various ethnic groups and kingdoms, each with distinct cultures and traditions. Bronzes, dated to about the 9th century C.E., were discovered in the 1940s at Igbo Ukwu, near Onitsha. Historians believed the copper and lead used to make the bronzes might have come from as far as Venice and India, the latter via trade routes through Egypt, the Nile valley, and the Chad basin.

Nok Terracotta Bas-relief Sculpture Source *https://www.pinterest.co.uk/*

West African powerful, sophisticated and influential empires or kingdoms/tribes dominated the area in and around Nigeria and there was extensive trading activity among them.

They include:

- the Yoruba city-states and kingdoms of Ife, Oyo, and Ijebu in the southwest;

- in the west, the Edo Benin empire;

- in the northern kingdom, the Islamic Kanim Borno empire;

- in the southeast, the Igbo kingdom of Onitsha;

- And the various Hausa-Fulani kingdoms, Hausa city-state and kingdoms of Katsina, Kano, Zaira, and Gobir in north-central Nigeria.

These empires controlled vast territories, and their rulers were able to establish centralised systems of government, taxation, and trade. Oyo, founded in the 14th century and located in the Savanna to the north of the forest, traded goods from the north—rock salt, copper, textiles, leather goods, and horses—with products from the south—kola nuts, indigo, parrots, and cowries. By the 17th Century, it had built up a cavalry force with which it dominated people in western Yorubaland. The history of Borno also antedates the 9th Century when Arabic writers in North Africa first noted the kingdom of Kanem, east of Lake Chad. The lake was much larger than the present-day body of water and its basin attracted settlements and encouraged exchange.

Queen Amina Mohamud was a Hausa warrior queen of the city-state Zazzau, presently in the North-West region of Nigeria. In the 16th Century, ruthless warrior Queen Amina commanded an army of 20,000 men and 1,000 cavalry troops and was well-trained and fearsome. She expanded the territory fourfold and surrounded her cities with earthen walls. These walls became commonplace across the nation until the British conquest of Zazzau in 1904;many of them survive today, known as Amina's walls.

The Nigeria that the first European explorers encountered in the 15th Century were home to various societies and cultures, including sprawling kingdoms and prosperous urban centres. The cities of Katsina and Kano in the northern part of now Nigeria each had populations of more than 100,000 people.

The Great Benin kingdom

The Great Benin kingdom is one of the oldest West African civilisations from 355 BC. The kingdom is recognised for its brilliant bronze, ivory, iron artefacts and military prowess.

A Benin Bronze plaque
in the British Museum

Aerial of Benin city (British Museum)

The old Benin City is still the present-day location of Benin City in Edo state, Southwest Nigeria. When the Europeans first arrived at the Benin kingdom in the late 15th Century, they were astonished by the wealth, quality of life and organisation.

The first set of Portuguese that came to Benin was astonished at this paradise in the middle of the African jungle made up of hundreds of interlocked cities and villages; they named it The Great City of Benin.

According to a Portuguese ship captain Lourenco Pinto in 1691, *"Benin was larger than Lisbon (the Capital City of Portugal), wealthy, dynamic and well-governed to the extent that there was no theft"*.

The Dutch writer Olfert Dapper also wrote: *"Benin City is at least four miles wide. The city has wide, straight roads lined by houses. The houses are large and handsome, with walls made from clay. The people are very friendly, and there seems to be no stealing..... It is large and square and surrounded by a wall. The court is divided into many palaces with separate houses and apartments for courtiers"*.

Houses and streets were highly organised in a mathematical pattern unknown to Europeans at the time. Benin was one of the first ancient cities to have some kind of street light. These were huge metal lamps placed around the city with a wick fuelled by palm oil to illuminate them at night.

Massive walls and deep ditches surrounded Benin City, which stretched beyond the city walls. Work on the fortification first began around 800 AD and continued up until around 1460. Upon completion, the structure comprised ditches and ramparts and enclosed about 6,500 square kilometres of community land of more than 500 interconnected villages. The new official length of the Wall of Benin was 21,196 kilometres, announced in 2012

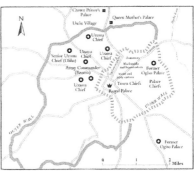

A street in Benin City
in the late 18th Century

Aerial map of the Benin Walls.
Source *https://thinkafrica.net/*

The Great Wall of Benin was twice the length of the Ming Great Wall of China, which measured only 8,851 kilometres. The Benin Wall made the Guinness Book of World Records in 1974 as the world's most extensive human earthworks before the mechanical era. In 1995, it was also recognised in the cultural category of the UNESCO World Heritage Tentative list.

Before colonisation, literacy was widespread in many regions of Nigeria, and business was thriving. Luxury goods were traded from Bornu's (north-eastern Nigeria) kingdom to as far as Venice, the Silk Road and the Maldive Islands.

2.1. THE HISTORY OF THE SLAVE TRADE IN NIGERIA

The act of slavery is as old as humanity itself. The concept of slavery has been around throughout the European Middle Ages, with the Crusades between Christians and Muslims giving an added excuse for enslaving people. It was not uncommon to find the practice in some societies, such as China, Burma and India, but there was never any timespan when slavery was the dominant mode of production in Asia.

The cultural set-up of the people of the West African coasts is no different from that time – it accepted slavery. Nigeria was no exception; the traditional slave trade had been part and parcel of Africa before the arrival of Europeans. Obtaining captives on African soil was done through inter-tribal and communal warfare. That is, kings fought their neighbours and subdued prisoners. Typically, in ancient Africa, when someone was captured at war, he served as a slave fora very short time. Captives or their offspring were then absorbed as ordinary members of society, especially if they had a skill or could prove valuable. There was no scope for the continual abuse of man by man in Africa during this period. The Arabs were the first to introduce the perpetual exploitation of slaves during the Trans-Sahara slavery in East Africa and Sudan when Arabs took many Africans to Arab countries and Asia.

The intervention of European and American ships in the 17th century and the offering of trading goods in exchange for people increased the demand for lots of slaves. The demand dissolved the continent's ethical slave conventions that had governed slavery for centuries, leading to the 'degradation of slavery' and an added incentive for Africa to enslave each other.

Inter-tribal and communal warfare

African war commandant

Transatlantic slavery could never have happened without African collaboration. Some rulers or wealthy and influential merchants in Nigeria who were more concerned about their selfish interests joined to make slavery possible for the Europeans. They facilitated the movement of slaves from inland to the port and the Europeans loaded and shipped the slaves to America. Initially, these rulers found European goods sufficiently desirable to hand over captives they had taken from warfare. However, by the mid-17th Century, the European demand for captives, particularly for the sugar plantations in the Americas, became so great that sufficient slaves could only be acquired through kidnapping, raiding and warfare. Some societies preyed on others to obtain captives in exchange for European firearms. If they did not acquire firearms in this way to protect themselves, they would be attacked and captured by their rivals and enemies who did possess such weapons. Europeans took advantage of this situation and started playing African leaders, equipping them to challenge each other to obtain more slaves. Eventually, Europe benefited from whichever of the two nations won the conflict.

Following the capture of slaves inland, the captives were marched from the inland of Nigeria to the coast. The harsh reality of the slave caravans was written by the British explorer Mungo Park in the 1790s. "..... *a typical column of slaves would spend eight hours a day on the road, covering about 20 miles. They were joined in pairs at the leg, and a chain would attach them, one to another, at the neck"*.... *'they are doomed to a life of captivity in a foreign land'.*

Slave trade in Lagos   Badagry slave market

During the slave trade era, the Badagry region, due to the large expanse of water, served as a place for the Europeans to harbour their slave ships. In Lagos, the slave trade was in vogue, and the wealthy and powerful Nigerian controlled human beings as enslaved people. Lagos became a slave port, where buying and selling people as slaves were carried out. There was also a slave market where bargaining was done and slave fort buildings located in different areas where slaves were examined, sorted and kept until they were transported to the ship in the open seas.

Slaves are inspected before boarding

Most of the captives resisted being transported to the ships lying at anchor on the open seas. One slave-ship captain, Thomas Phillips, left this account: "*When our slaves came to the seaside, our canoes were ready to carry them off to the longboat if the sea permitted, and she conveyed them aboard ship, where the men were all put in irons, two and two shackled together, to prevent their mutiny or swimming ashore. The negroes are so wilful and loathe to leave their own country that they have often leapt out of canoes, boats and ships into the sea and kept underwater till they drowned to avoid being taken up and saved ... They having a more dreadful apprehension of Barbados than we (British)were of hell ...*"

Slave Ship Stock Photos and Pictures | Getty Images

The average slaving voyage to the Americas took six to eight weeks. The ships' crews used iron muzzles and whips to exert control. The slaves were chained together on two tiers of shelves with less than 1 metre (100 cm) in which to sit up. Male slaves were usually shackled together at the foot. In theory, each man was allotted a space of 1.8m (6ft) by 0.4m (1ft 4in).

Sailors playing with a female slave

Branding of slave with a hot iron. Source: *www.vox.com*

The separation of male and female slaves and the levels of violence and aggression aboard slave ships made acts of physical and sexual abuse by the sailors a feature of all voyages. Food consisted mostly of starch: biscuit, flour, yam and beans flavoured with palm oil and hot peppers.

The loss of life was high on all voyages, particularly during the first part, when disease and psychological trauma were especially lethal. When the disease began to spread, there was a tendency to throw the sicker Africans overboard. An estimated 5 million Africans – 30% of all those transported – perished before they reached the Americas.

A 2014 estimate based on the slave voyages database suggests the number of slaves transported across the Atlantic from Nigeria was approximately 5.7 million of the 12.5 million African slaves.

Another study in the United States, Latin America, and Western Europe involving the DNA of 50,281 African American people revealed that Nigeria was the most common country of origin for most black people tested.

Nigeria became a significant point of export of slaves from Africa to the Americas during the 17th and 18th centuries. Most people captured as slaves from Nigeria were likely to have been Igbo or Yoruba. According to some historians, the Igbo were characterised by high rates of rebellion and suicide as they resisted and fought back against enslavement. The Yoruba had traditional, cultural identification marks (tribal marks), such as tattoo and scarification designs. These assisted those kidnapped and enslaved people who escaped to locate other members of their ethnic group. In the colonies, European slavers tried to dissuade the practice of traditional tribal customs. They also mixed people of different ethnic groups to make it more difficult for them to communicate and band together in rebellion.

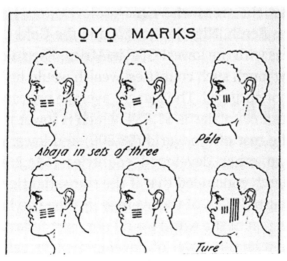

Yoruba tribal mark

tunes and woes irrespective of who you are. Before Colonialism, the axe of Sango (God of Thunder) was the gavel, and the square of Esu (death) was the court. No one would despise the palm font leaves Ogun (God of iron) wore as the magistrate's wig.

Many examples abound of the heavy emphasis on accountability and good governance across several pre-colonial African communities. Among the Yoruba of southwestern Nigeria, the institution of Oyo-Mesi, the King making body, acted as a check against the abuse of power by the King of Oyo. The Alaafin was constrained to rule with caution and respect for his subjects. When the King is proven to have undermined the interests of his subjects, such as gross miscarriage of justice for personal gains, the Oyo-Mesi will present him with an empty calabash or parrot's egg as a sign that he must commit suicide since he could not be deposed, according to tradition.

In the Igbo acephalous society, the absence of an overarching authority placed leadership in the hands of the people – the very epitome of accountability and good governance. The titled chiefs sat together to address the more complex governance issues. There is a saying among the Igbo, *'onye akpọrọ anaghị agha ụgha' that is a 'titled man does not lie.* If one wanted to hear the truth and to be granted pristine justice according to the prevailing standards, he only needed to get the impeccable body of titled men to listen to the case in question.

Numerous examples abound across Nigerian culture. What held these communities together and brought administrative corruption down to the barest minimum was a set of rules and regulations, agreed principles and moral values packaged in spiritual terms (sanction and consequences) to ensure social justice and compliance.

3. The Colonisation of Nigeria

Before 1700s, the British Empire and other European powers' settlements were restricted to the coast of Africa. They could not establish colonies in Africa because of the health threat posed by malaria and yellow fever in the heart of Africa. Only one in ten survived malaria and yellow fever. During this period, the Europeans called Africa the "White Man's Grave." However, some factors happened at the turn of the 1800s that enabled the colonisation of Africa by the Europeans. Firstly, the discovery of quinine against malaria allowed the European powers to move inside and settle down within the continent. Secondly, Europeans started sending explorers to Africa, recording and sending information about the continent's wealth to their financiers, who began to elicit more interest in the continent. Thirdly, the innovation of the steam engine and iron-hulled boats enabled Europeans to explore the inland part of the continent through rivers. For example, Mungo Park explored the rivers Niger and Benue. Fourthly, European powers were in political competition, with each European country trying to assert dominance. They decided instead of fighting each other for lands in Europe, they should come and take as much land as they wanted in Africa. Finally, the end of the slave trade created a financial vacuum that capitalists were desperate to fill. Therefore, when explorers reported the discovery of raw materials on the continent, capitalists saw an opportunity for a new "legal" trade. The Europeans also wanted to use the African population for marketing their manufactured goods.

Following the abolition of the slave trade, many of the slaves exported in the 1820s were intercepted by the ships of the Royal Navy, emancipated, and deposited in Sierra Leone under missionary tutelage. Some of these slaves began migrating back from Sierra Leone to their homeland, and many invited missionaries to follow them. In the 1840s, these ex-slaves made themselves available as agents who allowed missionaries and British traders to access such places as Lagos, Abeokuta, Calabar, Lokoja, Onitsha, Brass, and Bonny.

Initially, the British were unwilling to assume the expense of maintaining an administration in Nigeria. To reduce costs, Lagos was administered first from Freetown in Sierra Leone, along with Gold Coast forts such as Elmina, and later from Accra (in present-day Ghana); only in 1886 did Lagos become a separate colony. The British began increasing their influence by imposing a Crown Colony government on Nigeria in 1807. British influence in the Niger area increased gradually over the 19th century, but Britain did not effectively occupy the area until 1885 when other European powers acknowledged Britain's dominance over the Nigeria colony at the 1885 Berlin Conference.

Before olonialism, Nigeria was composed of a lot of very small units. These were not necessarily formal nations like today's modern formation, but there were agreements, conventions, and boundaries that the people were aware of and respected. These units corresponded to different ethnic groups. However, during the Berlin Conference, the Europeans drew the partitioning lines mainly for the Europeans' economic benefit. They did not try to consider any ethnic groups and where their boundary might start or finish.

British Prime Minister Lord Salisbury duly captured the arbitrariness of the partitioning exercise. He said: *"We have been engaged in drawing lines on upon maps of a continent where no white man's feet have ever trod. We have been giving away to ourselves mountains and rivers and lakes, only hindered by the small impediment that we never knew exactly where the mountains and rivers and lakes were.".*

However, the partitions were enforced as the national boundaries of Africa throughout the colonisation period, so most of the partitions persisted long after the colonial powers left Africa.

The consequence of the partitions was that, in most African countries like Nigeria, a significant fraction (around 40-45%) of the population grouped together into the same national border had nothing in common. Some historical enemies were lumbered together. The partitions have led to above-average ethnic conflicts in Sub-Saharan Africa since independence. These wars and conflicts are why most of these independent African countries failed to develop their economy. The frequency and intensity of these conflicts have lowered the incentive for economic development. It destroyed wealth and made it difficult for African countries to implement reforms and build institutions.

The recent conflict between the Fulani herders and the arable farmers in northern Nigeria was rooted in the amalgamation of two existing British colonial states that had nothing in common (language or religion). The Protectorate of Northern Nigeria and the Colony and Protectorate of Southern Nigeria created the Nigerian state in 1914.

The empirical result from the research based on the 43,000 reported conflicts in Africa from 1997 to 2000 has shown that the ethnic map of Africa drawn by the Europeans was very bad for peace and the development of Africa.

Below are the findings on Africa and its civil wars.

- Civil conflict in Africa is concentrated in historical homelands of partitioned ethnicities.

- Civil conflict intensity is 50% higher in countries where partitioned ethnicities reside. That means it worsens if a region or partition splits an ethnicity between two fighting countries.

- Violence against civilians is also 40% higher.

- 10% higher chance of control change, e. g., organisation of a coup.

The British Empire took over Nigeria in many ways. Firstly, the British established control over the country through military means. Secondly, they exerted economic control over Nigeria by investing in infrastructure that allowed them to access and exploit its resources. Finally, they exerted political control by installing a puppet government loyal to the British Crown.

Even though many Nigerian citizens today are nostalgic for the Empire, Colonialism has little benevolent intent and many disastrous consequences. Even though independence has come a long way since colonial rule, Colonial interference still has repercussions.

Following the Berlin Conference, the Royal Niger Company led the way to colonise what later became known as Nigeria and signed 237 separate treaties with local rulers between December 1884 and October 1886 alone, which they later broke. The Royal Navy bombarded Lagos in November 1851, ousted the pro-slavery Oba Kosoko and established a treaty with the newly installed Oba Akintoye, who was expectedly more amenable to British interests. Lagos was annexed as a Crown Colony in 1861 via the Lagos Treaty of Cession.

Following the bombardment, other chiefs quickly signed over their land and legal authority to the company in return for being allowed to farm and maintain their laws. The company initially declared that it had no 'desire to interfere more than is essential with the internal arrangements of the Chiefs of Central Africa, but the company went against its word'.

The Royal Niger Company's charter was revoked and the territory, known as Nigeria, was sold to the British government for £865,000 (at today's exchange rate of £46,407,250 (NGN 50,386,455,032,400).

The British then led a series of military campaigns to enlarge its sphere of influence and expand its commercial opportunities in the Lagos colony. By 1893, the British conquered the rest of Yorubaland, which had also been weakened by sixteen years of civil war. In the name of liberating the Igbos from the Aro Confederacy, the British launched the Anglo-Aro War of 1901–1902. But the British had difficulty conquering Igboland, which lacked a central political organisation. The British forces later began annual pacification missions to convince the locals of British supremacy. A campaign against the Sokoto Caliphate began in 1900 with the creation of the Protectorate of Northern Nigeria. The British captured Kano in 1903.

In 1906 the British merged the small Lagos Colony and the Southern Nigeria Protectorate into a new Colony of Southern Nigeria, and in 1914 that was combined with the Northern Nigeria Protectorate to form the Colony and Protectorate of Nigeria at the urging of Governor Frederick Lugard. This Protectorate lasted until 1960 and gave Britain total control over Nigeria's economy, foreign affairs and defence. Britain also began to impose its own values and governing structures on Nigeria, which led to increased tension and conflict between the two cultures. The British imposed heavy taxation due to their strict control over a single British-controlled currency.

The primary purpose of Colonialism by the British was to systematically take out Nigerian's wealth using Nigeria's labour and raw material to generate profit and eventually transfer it to Britain's mother countries. The corporations under Colonialism only paid an extremely small wage to farmers, which was below minimum wage, usually barely sufficient to keep the worker physically alive. As a result, on top of working for the Colonials, most farmers had to return to the land and farm staple foods to feed their families and pay taxes imposed on them. The farmers were also forced to produce cash crops such as rubber, cocoa, groundnut, palm oil, etc., as opposed to staple foods to acquire money to afford European goods, such as tools, clothing, and bicycles. In addition, they had to pay taxes imposed on their cattle, land, houses, and themselves. The consequence was that while most Nigerian farmers struggled to feed themselves from their agricultural activities, the raw materials produced on their farms were used to develop Europe.

In addition, other none European business people flourished during Colonialism. For example, in Nigeria, the Lebanese and Syrians became the intermediaries between the British and the farmers. They became household names in Nigeria, e. g. the Raccah and Leventis, Madhvani and Visram in Africa.

In Britain, the port of Liverpool was the first to switch to importing palm oil and other peasant-produced raw materials early in the 19th century when the slave trade ended. This was a paradigm shift from exploiting African labour from another part of the world to exploiting Africa's labour and raw materials inside Africa.

3.1. **THE STORY OF MR LEVER, A SHOPKEEPER**

In 1885, during Colonialism, one shrewd businessman, William H. Lever, had just started a soap-making factory, 'Sunlight', in Liverpool, England. Most agricultural raw materials used to make the soap did not grow in the U.K. and were cultivated and harvested in Nigeria: palm oil, palm kernel oil, groundnut oil, and copra. Europe had just carved up and condemned Africa as the raw material reservoir for Europe. Mr Lever took advantage of the opportunity and within ten years his company was selling 40,000 tons of soap per year in England, which increased to 80,000 tons of soap. He later expanded his business to Europe and North America.

In 1910, Lever acquired three small companies in Nigeria, Sierra Leone and Liberia and established himself in key British Colonies in West Africa. In 1920, the shopkeeper bought the Niger Company for £8 million through his profitable investment in Africa and and partnered with his competitor to become the United Africa Company (UAC). By the end of the Colonial period, Unilever had become a worldwide household name, selling traditional soaps, detergents, margarine, lard, ghee, cooking oil, canned foods, candles, glycerine, oil cake, and toiletries such as toothpaste. In 1929, UAC drastically reduced palm oil prices paid to farmers in Nigeria while increasing imported goods' costs. This cunning move helped UAC during the depression to make £6,302,875 and pay a dividend of 15% on ordinary shares.

This story follows the trail of how everybody benefited during British Colonialism in Nigeria, the citizens and the businesses in the U.K., the trading companies, Her Majesty's Revenue & Customs (U.K. tax office), banks, and insurance companies — only the Nigerian farmers failed to benefit.

In Europe, during the 18th and 19th centuries, agriculture was heavily transformed through the intensive application of scientific knowledge and research to irrigation, fertilisers, tools, crop selection, stock breeding, etc. It is amazing that despite the revolution of agriculture in Europe, the Colonialists deliberately decided not to transfer this knowledge and change agricultural production technology in Nigeria. This single act proved that the Europeans did not intend to modernise Africa during Colonialism. Most Nigerian farmers were tilling the land with a hoe and cutlass at the beginning of slavery and Colonialism – and were still doing the same 400 years later.

3.2. BENEFIT EFFECTS OF BRITISH COLONIALISM ON NIGERIANS

This section would not be complete without looking at the positive aspects of Colonialism in Nigeria. The British erected some infrastructures while they were in Nigeria. They include railways, seaports, airports, roads, and hospitals. The end-users are the Nigerians after independence; before this, most Africans would walk long distances, which could delay achieving different agendas. The British-built road network enabled people from various cultures and ethnicities to interact and correspond better.

The British style of governance also facilitated dialogue among tribes, reduced unrest and tribal wars within many African countries and proposed peace on many issues. Before Colonisation, Nigerians experienced many infant and childhood deaths, yet they were unaware of the causes of the fatalities. The Colonists coming to Africa brought a better healthcare sector and reduced infant deaths. The southern part of Nigeria was one of the Colonial areas that received most social services from the British. For example, Ibadan, one of Africa's most heavily populated cities, had 34 hospital beds for half a million blacks. It was worse in other colonies, which had 40 million African to 52 beds in other African countries.

Before Colonisation, many Nigerians were illiterates who did not know how to read and write, but the arrival of the British paved the way for education to gain historical insights into Africa and formalised vocational training. Many of Nigeria's astute readers and professors are children of farmers privileged to study in the nations of their Colonial masters.

The Colonisation introduced many other social activities, infrastructures, and amenities in the cities of Nigeria, like pipe-borne water, security, and some advancement in today's social environment. Most of these facilities were established primarily in cities and ports where most Europeans settled in Nigeria. The era of Colonialism also favoured women, who were protected mainly from prejudice and assaults and allowed to express their views publicly.

On the positive side, the church did help to reduce some negative African cultural and religious manifestations, such as the killing of twins.

3.3. THE COLONISATION OF NIGERIA WAS NOT A WALK IN THE PARK

The Colonisation of Nigeria was not a walk in the park for the British, and there was a lot of resistance to British rule. The people of Nigeria waged a series of uprisings, rebellions, and wars against the British Empire. The resistance began with the first major uprising in 1807, led by the Igbo people in the southeast. This was followed by a decade of wars and rebellions, culminating in the 1868 war led by the Yoruba people in the southwest. The British eventually conquered Nigeria and ruled it as a Colony for nearly a century. However, the people of Nigeria continued to resist British rule throughout the Colonial period. The most significant resistance movement was the Nigerian independence movement, which culminated in the country's independence in 1960.

King Jaja of Opobo (1821–1891) was the first king of Opobo in the present-day River State of Nigeria. Jaja earned his way out of servanthood (apprenticeship) after serving his master for some years. He later took charge of the trades and turned Opobo into a prominent trading post in the region's palm oil trade. Jaja barred entry to Europeans, effectively monopolising trade, and by 1870 was selling eight thousand tons of palm oil directly to the British. Opobo also shipped palm oil directly to Liverpool.

At the 1884 Berlin Conference on Africa's partition, the Europeans designated Opobo as British territory. However, King Jaja refused to cease taxing British traders. In 1887, Jaja was cunningly invited by the British consul to discuss allowing British traders access to all parts of his kingdom. During the meeting, he was threatened to follow the British consul to Accra or allow Opobo to be destroyed by the British naval guns. Jaja had no choice but to save his people and follow the consul to Accra.

King Jaja was arrested and exiled to the island of Saint Vincent, where he lived in obscurity for the rest of his life. Despite his downfall, his legacy lived on. Many Nigerians revere him as a symbol of resistance against Colonialism and a champion of African independence.

Ovonramwen Nogbaisi (ruled 1888 – 1897), was the Oba (King) of the Kingdom of Benin. At the end of the 19th century, the Kingdom of Benin retained its independence and monopoly over the palm oil, rubber and ivory trade. The British wanted the Benin Empire's annexation and the Oba's removal so that they could access the city's rich natural resources.

A British invasion force headed by Phillips was sent out to overthrow the Oba in 1896. Phillips planned to gain access to Ovonramwen's palace by announcing that he intended to negotiate. The force's weapons were hidden in baggage, with troops disguised as bearers. Ovonramwen's messengers warned the British not to violate Benin's territorial sovereignty, claiming he could not see Phillips due to ceremonial duties. Phillips sent his stick to the Oba, a deliberate insult designed to provoke the conflict that would provide an excuse for British annexation.

British ransacking Benin Palace

Phillip's expedition was later ambushed and killed. Subsequently, a military operation against Benin in 1897 led by Ha ry Rawson resulted in the burning of Benin City, the dest tion and looting of the royal palaces, and the deaths of ' inhabitants, including men, women and children. O wen escaped but returned to the city to formally surrender on 5 August 1897. Ovonramwen was exiled to Calabar and died in 1914.

Ekumeku Resistance Movement The Colonialism and invasion of British troops in 1901 was a catastrophe for the ingenious Igbo African way of life, but the Ekumeku underground resistance movement attempted to right the wrong. Ekumeku War between the British and the people in the Asaba hinterland lasted until 1911.

The Women's War, or Aba Women's Protest, was a period of unrest in Colonial Nigeria in November 1929. The protests broke out when thousands of Igbo women travelled to Oloko town to protest against the Warrant Chiefs. African women built upon these reforms, which have been seen as a prelude to the emergence of mass African nationalism.

Madame Nwanyeruwa. The market women, led by an iconic woman named Nwanyeruwa Oleka Okpo organised themselves and challenged the authority of the British government. The British officials responded by firing Lewis rapid-fire guns with its 97-round quick-fire magazines against 300 women. 54 women were killed, and 57 were wounded.

Alimotu Pelewura (1865–1951) was a Nigerian trader who led the Lagos Market Women's Association. She was also an important political ally of Herbert Macaulay.

Funmilayo Anikulapo-Kuti was a Nigerian educator and women's rights activist. During the 1940s, she established the Abeokuta Women's Union and led the protests of 10,000 women. She died at 77 after being wounded in a military raid on family property. Ransome-Kuti's children included the musician Fela Kuti, doctor and activist Beko Ransome-Kuti, and health minister Olikoye Ransome-Kuti.

4. Nigerian Independence

After the First World War, the British struggled to keep control of their Nigerian colony until she became independent in 1960. Beginning in the 1920s, many Nigerians joined other Blacks in various parts of the world to embark on the broader project of Pan-Africanism, which sought to liberate Black people from racism and European domination.

By 1922, the National Council of British West Africa, an organisation consisting of elites across West Africa, was asking for a proportional representative, with 50% of the members of the Legislative Council being Nigerians. In 1923 Herbert Macaulay, the grandson of Samuel Ajayi Crowther, established the first Nigerian political party, the Nigerian National Democratic Party, which successfully contested three Lagos seats in the Legislative Council. Macaulay became the "father of modern Nigerian nationalism." The council also demanded a university in West Africa and more senior positions for Nigerians in the Colonial civil service.

Nnamdi Azikiwe — After the 1930s, political activities focused primarily on ways to end British rule. A national party, the Nigerian Youth Movement, emerged in 1934, and its members won elections to the Legislative Council. After 1940, political activities were broadened to include more people. In 1944, Herbert Macaulay and Nnamdi Azikiwe, an Igbo educated in the United States, united more than 40 different groups to establish the National Council of Nigeria and the Cameroons (NCNC). The forces unleashed against the British were now diverse, including soldiers who had served in World War II, the media, restless youths, market women, educated people, and farmers, all of whom became committed to the anti-colonial movement. Political leaders resorted to using political parties and the media to mobilise millions of Nigerians against the continuation of British rule. In response to Azikiwe and other nationalists, the Lyttelton constitution of 1954 created a federal system comprising the three geographic regions of Nigeria, the Southern Cameroons, and the Federal Territory of Lagos.

Obafemi Awolowo — In 1954, Nigeria became a federal state with three regions, the Western, Eastern, and Northern regions. Internal self-government was granted to the Western and Eastern regions in 1957. The Eastern region was dominated by Azikiwe, and the Western one by Chief Obafemi Awolowo, a Yoruba lawyer who founded the Action Group in 1950. While the Eastern and Western regions demanded immediate self-government, the Northern People's Congress (NPC), composed mainly of northerners and headed by Abubakar Tafawa Balewa, was not ready for internal self-government. They needed time to catch up with the educationally advanced south.

In early 1950, Mr Harold McMillan, a British Prime Minister, called African Independence a long and overdue *"wind of change sweeping through colonial Anglophone and Francophone Africa."* The people's yearning for independence was so great that the colonisers could no longer ignore it.

In 1959, the end of the British Colonial system in Ghana led to seventeen African countries' freedom the following year.

Nigeria Independent day

Nigeria's independence

Nigeria was granted independence on October 1, 1960. Independence Day was celebrated with pride, pomp, pageantry, nationwide festivities, and excitement in the belief that Africa had finally turned a corner.

The NCNC, now headed by Azikiwe, formed a coalition with Balewa's NPC after neither party won a majority in the 1959 elections. Balewa continued to serve as the prime minister, a position he had held since 1957, while Azikiwe took the largely ceremonial position of president of the Senate.

After a brief honeymoon period, Nigeria's long-standing regional stresses, caused by ethnic competitiveness, educational inequality, and economic imbalance, again came to the fore in the controversial census of 1962–63. The country was segmented into three large geographic regions, each essentially controlled by an ethnic group—the west by the Yoruba, the east by the Igbo, and the north by the Hausa-Fulani.

Conflicts became endemic as regional leaders protected their privileges; the south complained of northern domination and the north feared that the southern elite was bent on capturing power. The point of no return was reached in January 1966, when, after the collapse of order in the west following the fraudulent election of October 1965, a group of army officers attempted to overthrow the federal government and Prime Minister Balewa and two of the regional premiers were murdered. A military administration was set up under Maj. Gen. Johnson Aguiyi-Ironsi's plan to abolish the regions and impose a unitary government was met with anti-Igbo riots in the north. The military intervention worsened the political situation. The army also split along ethnic lines, its officers clashed over power, and the instigators and leaders of the coup were accused of favouring Igbo domination. In July 1966, northern officers staged a countercoup: Aguiyi-Ironsi and Lieut were assassinated. Col. Yakubu Gowon came to power. Intercommunal clashes in the north and threats of secession in the south compounded the crisis.

4.1. THE CIVIL WAR

On May 30, 1967, Ojukwu declared the secession of the three states of the Eastern region under the name of the Republic of Biafra, which the federal government interpreted as an act of rebellion. Fighting broke out in early July and escalated into a full-scale civil war within weeks. In August, Biafran troops crossed the Niger, seized Benin City, and were on their way to Lagos before being checked at Ore, a small town in the Western state (now Ondo state). Shortly after that, federal troops entered Enugu, the provisional capital of Biafra, and penetrated the Igbo heartland. The next two years were marked by stiff resistance in the shrinking Biafran enclave and by heavy casualties among civilians and both armies. Peace-making attempts by the Organization of African Unity (now the African Union) remained ineffective. At the same time, Biafra began earning recognition from African states and secured aid from international organisations for a starving population.

The final Biafran collapse began on December 24, 1969, when federal troops launched a massive effort at a time when Biafra was short on ammunition, and its people were desperate for food. Ojukwu fled to Côte d'Ivoire on January 11, 1970, and a Biafran deputation formally surrendered in Lagos four days later.

The war cost Nigeria approximately 13 million lives, mostly from starvation and disease, considerable money and world prestige. The end of the Nigeria-Biafra civil war yielded the official policy of 'Reconciliation, Reconstruction and Rehabilitation', otherwise referred to as the three R's, and was meant to reintegrate the rebel and secessionist Biafra region into the bigger Nigerian federation. Reconstruction after the war was swift, although the Ibos felt they had been displaced from their job positions, during the war, by other Nigerians. Feelings of injustice were also caused by a change of currency, rendering pre-war supplies in Biafra worth much less than their real value. However, fifty years later, indicators show that this policy failed to resolve the issues that led to the war, notably grievances on injustice, marginalization, alienation, flawed federalism, and inappropriate sectional domination.

4.2. THE SECOND REPUBLIC

The oil boom that followed the war allowed the federal government to finance development programs and consolidate its power. Gowon was overthrown in July 1975 and fled to Great

Britain. The new head of state, Brig. Gen. Murtala Ramat Mohammed initiated many changes during his brief time in office: he initiated the process for a return to civilian rule. He was assassinated in February 1976 during an unsuccessful coup attempt, and his top aide, Lieut. Gen. Olusegun Obasanjo became head of the government and pursued Mohammed's desire to return the country to civilian rule. Shehu Shagari, the dominant party's NPN candidate, won the 1979 presidential election, defeating Chief Obafemi Awolowo.

The NPN's party leaders used their political power to gain access to public treasuries and distribute privileges to their followers. Public members were angry and many openly challenged the relevance of a democracy that could not produce leaders who would improve their lives and provide moral authority. Shagari could not manage the political crisis that followed or end Nigeria's continuing economic decline and the military seized the opportunity to stage a coup on December 31, 1983 that brought Maj. Gen. Muhammad Buhari to power.

Military regimes, 1983–99

Buhari justified his coup and subsequent actions by citing the troubles of the Second Republic and the declining economy. The regime declared a "War Against Indiscipline" (WAI), which resulted in several politicians' arrests, detentions, and jailings. Gen. Ibrahim Babangida assumed power following a bloodless coup in August 1985. Babangida initially presented the image of an affectionate and considerate leader to the public and the media. He released political detainees and promised that public opinion would influence his decisions and those of the Armed Forces Ruling Council, the supreme governing body. The public, however, demanded an end to military rule. Babangida outwardly supported a return to civilian government but worked to undermine the process to retain power.

A presidential election was slated for June 1993 between two pro-government candidates: Chief M.K.O. Abiola of the SDP and Alhaji Bashir Tofa of the NRC. Contrary to government expectations, the election was held on schedule and was free, fair, and peaceful. Chief Abiola won, but Babangida annulled the results before they became official.

If the political future of Nigeria appeared bright with the victory of Chief Abiola in June 1993, Abacha's seizure of power and subsequent rule reversed most of the gains the country had made since 1960. Abacha's reign was so bad that the public began to question the existence of Nigeria as a political entity.

| Gen Babangida | Moshood Abiola |

Many leading politicians called for the country's breakup and advocated a confederacy with a weakened centre and a divided army and police force. The country's international image was damaged and it suffered serious condemnation

The decisive turning point in military disengagement came with Abacha's sudden death in June 1998. Gen. Abdulsalam Abubakar, appointed to replace him, promised to transfer power to civilians. He freed political prisoners, ended the harassment of political opponents, and set forth a timetable for the transition to civilian rule.

4.3. RETURN TO CIVILIAN RULE — THE 1999 ELECTIONS

After Abacha's death, political activity blossomed as numerous parties were formed. Of these, three emerged that could contest elections: the People's Democratic Party (PDP), the Alliance for Democracy, and the All People's Party. The presidential election took place in February, and Olusegun Obasanjo of the PDP, head of state 1976–79, was declared the winner.

Nigeria under Olusegun Obasanjo

Obasanjo was sworn in on May 29, 1999. Although the general conditions in Nigeria improved under Obasanjo, there was still considerable strife. Ethnic conflict—previously kept in check during military rule—erupted in various parts of Nigeria. The friction increased between Muslims and Christians when some northern and central states adopted Islamic law (the Sharī'ah). Demonstrations were held to protest the government's oil policies and high fuel prices. Residents of the Niger delta also protested the operations of petroleum companies in their area, asserting that the companies exploited their land while not providing a reasonable share of the petroleum profits in return. Their protests evolved into coordinated militant action in 2006. Petroleum companies were targeted: their employees were kidnapped, and refineries and pipelines were damaged as militants attempted to disrupt oil production and inflict economic loss.

Obasanjo was also faced with resolving an ongoing border dispute with neighbouring Cameroon that included the question of which country had rights to the Bakassi Peninsula, an oil-rich area. Under the terms of a 2002 International Court of Justice ruling, the region was awarded to Cameroon; Obasanjo eventually honoured the terms of the ruling in 2006 and withdrew its forces.

Meanwhile, Obasanjo was the subject of domestic and international criticism for his attempt to amend the constitution to allow him to stand for a third term as president; the Senate rejected the proposed amendment in 2006.

Yar'Adua, Umaru Musa

Umaru Musa Yar'Adua won the presidential poll in April 2007. However, Yar'Adua's health was the subject of rumours, as he had travelled abroad for medical treatment several times before his presidency. His ability to serve as president was questioned after he went to Saudi Arabia in late November 2009 for a long time to treat heart and kidney problems. While he was absent from Nigeria for several weeks, there were calls for Yar'Adua to transfer power to the vice president, Goodluck Jonathan formally.

The 2011 elections

Jonathan was the overwhelming presidential election winner, receiving almost 59 per cent of the vote among a field of 19 other challengers.

Rise of Boko Haram — Among the most-pressing concerns in Jonathan's first full term as president was the ongoing threat presented by Boko Haram, an Islamic sectarian movement founded in 2002 in north-eastern Nigeria; the group imposed

Sharī'ah or Islamic law. In April 2014, Boko Haram's mass kidnapping of more than 275 girls from a boarding school in Chibok in Borno state brought the group and its unabated campaign of terror into the international spotlight and was widely condemned across the globe.

The 2015 elections and electorate concerns

The government's inability to eliminate the threat of Boko Haram and the persistent complaint of corruption were key issues in the run-up to the 2015 presidential election: Despite overall economic growth during Jonathan's term, many Nigerians, especially those in rural areas and in the north, lived in poverty. The election was the most closely contested ever in Nigeria; Jonathan conceded when it became clear that Buhari had won. Buhari was inaugurated on May 29, 2015.

Nigeria under Buhari

Buhari faced several challenges as president. In 2016, declining oil revenue led to Nigeria's first recession in over 25 years. Although some recovery progress was evident by 2018, many Nigerian citizens did not see relief. The country earned the unenviable distinction that year of having the world's most people in extreme poverty. Many questioned whether Buhari was fit enough to serve as president, as he repeatedly left the country for medical treatment of an undisclosed ailment; in 2017, he was absent for several months. Buhari was re-elected and inaugurated for his second term on May 29, 2019.

4.4. THE MILLENNIAL AND GENERATION Z 2023 GENERAL ELECTION

General Elections to elect a new President, Federal and State Legislators and Governors are scheduled for February 2023.

Many researchers believe that the Millennials and Generation Z have come of age in Nigeria Politics and their impact will be felt in the 2023 General Election.

Millennials, born between 1981 and 1996, aged between 25 and 35, make up 39% of Nigeria's consumer market and have a lot of power in purchasing decisions. They are often called the "lost generation" due to the significant social, economic, and political changes they have experienced. Despite these challenges, millennials in Nigeria are highly educated and ambitious, have high-value personal and professional development, and are skilled in technology. They are also socially conscious, actively engaged in social and political issues, and critical of the status quo.

Generation Z, was born between 1997 and 2012. Nigeria's age structure indicates that over 25% of its 200 million population belongs to Gen Z, which is characterized by their high technological savvy and comfort with digital technologies. They have grown up in a world of instant access to information and pervasive social media use. In Nigeria, Generation Z is faced with high unemployment and economic insecurity but is also the largest and most educated generation in the country's history. They are entrepreneurial, environmentally conscious, and embrace diversity and inclusivity.

Gen Zs were born during the dot com era and were raised on technology. They witnessed Barrack Obama's election, gender equality, sexual orientation equality, shared family responsibilities, and collective volunteerism. However, they were born into a deeply troubled system, a time of worldwide terrorism attacks, Arab uprisings, effects of climate change and a great recession. This generation has come of age to shape policies .

In Nigeria, both Millennials and Generation Z represent unique and dynamic generations that will shape the future of Nigeria in significant ways. They represent two distinct yet overlapping generations in Nigeria, accounting for nearly 60% of the population. Their diverse backgrounds, innovative spirits, and commitments make them poised to impact this General Election positively. They both embrace technology and digital communication. They are highly connected and use social media and other digital platforms to stay connected with friends, family, and professional networks. They are also comfortable using technology for work and are skilled at using digital tools to be productive and efficient. Researchers believe that in the 2023 General Election, they will live up to the clarion call that youths are the leaders of tomorrow by coming out in mass to vote for their leader.

Since independence, leadership in Nigeria has been portrayed as the right of the elderly. In Nigeria, the political culture is that wisdom is intrinsically associated with age. This was firmly enshrined in Nigerian political and economic policies where more than 75% of the population of Nigerian political leaders are above 60 years. More than 50% of them have been in power in one way or the other since the Second Republic when they, too, were youth.

The gerontocrats have made political participation and representation unattainable to Nigerian youth in two ways. Firstly, the cost of elections is so exorbitant that it is not attainable by honest young people except those sponsored by an old Nigerian politician. The financial barrier to contesting elections has made the opportunity for youth to hold political offices a mirage without compromising their integrity. Hence, we see many young politicians betraying their fellow youth once they are in power. Until now, the youth are regarded as angry dogs with no teeth that can only bark but not bite.

However, these youth recently realised the potential of harnessing and amplifying their voices through social media to demand good governance from the older generation. They have been able to express their unhappiness about the state of the country, which includes insecurities, uncontrolled and incessant killing and kidnapping, banditry, police brutality, poverty, unemployment, economic degeneration and political instability

For example, on October 22 2020, the anger of the youth of Nigeria kindled against the older politician, like that of Elihu against Job and his three older friends in the Bible book of Job chapter 32. The young man said, "*I had waited to speak, but I held back because you guys were older than me.*" He declared, "*I am young in years, while you are old; that is why I was timid and afraid to tell you what I know. I thought that age should speak and many years should teach wisdom. But there is a spirit within everyone (young or old), the breath of the Almighty, that makes them intelligent.*" He concluded from this experience in verse 9, "*Sometimes the elders are not wise. Sometimes the aged do not understand justice.*" (New Living Translation)

By coming to this realisation, the Nigerian youth organised and managed a protest against police brutality, the "END SARS" protest . Frightened by the cooperation of the youth that successfully managed the peaceful protest irrespective of their ethnic, religious and cultural differences, the government sent out thugs to infiltrate the process. The government disrupted the protest by sending the police and soldiers to kill 53 unarmed youths.

Many researchers say that during the presidential election in 2023, the Nigerian youth will harness their population and present themselves as a force to reckon with through their political activism by raising candidates that represent their will and aspiration for the future and by pursuing uncompromised prospects for good governance. They believe the youth will come out in large force and use their Permanent Voter's Card (PVC) to tackle the leadership monopoly of ageing Nigerian gerontocrats who have continuously undermined and sidelined the youth in Nigeria's political and economic climate.

The country's political and military leadership must therefore ensure a fair vote. All sides must respect the result. Then the international community needs to support Nigeria's efforts to promote economic growth and social inclusion, contain violence and extremism, and tackle corruption. Investment in diplomacy, economic engagement, and security will lead to a more prosperous Nigeria. Africa and the world will sleep better with a stable and peaceful Nigeria.

4.5. FACTORS THAT ACCOUNT FOR THE POLITICAL AND ECONOMIC STATE OF NIGERIA.

Firstly, Nigeria's government started a century ago under Colonial rule. The legacy of authoritarianism is inherent in the Colonial rule itself, which came suddenly upon the country, was imposed for a century on Nigerians, and ended abruptly when the population was unprepared. The Saylor Foundation points out that the 'Colonial administrative system was a top-down approach that was not geared towards the interest and well-being of those governed.' As a result, the unprepared Nigerian leaders were confronted with managing the newly independent country after independence. They found the bureaucratic-authoritarian tradition of the Colonial order and its autocratic policies more readily conducive to achieving their goals than democracy. As a result, within less than a decade, military rule and single-party or no-party governments became a common feature of Nigeria and the African political landscape.

Secondly, European colonisers did not adequately prepare Nigeria for democratic rule during Colonial rule, and the newly independent states had little time to prepare and plan postcolonial political governance. During independence, only 34,000 students of the 50 million people in Nigeria were enrolled in secondary schools, and there were only 160 physicians.

Thirdly, lack of adequate infrastructure. The roads and railroads built by the British were geographically designed and built to connect to the port areas to facilitate exports. Nigeria was not designed to have the manufacturing infrastructure to add value to its raw materials. The economy depends on agricultural trade, making them vulnerable to the international market.

Fourthly, historically, African independence happened around the Cold War after World War II. The Cold War was a period of geopolitical tension between the United States and the Soviet Union (the two superpowers) and their respective allies (the Western versus the Eastern Bloc). During this period, the superpower sponsors were more concerned about the leader's loyalty to either Washington or Moskow; democratic or dictatorial credentials of African leaders did not matter.

Fifthly, Nigeria received poor advice. World Bank senior vice-president Ernest Stern admitted that the western countries gave Nigeria poor and bad advice. *"We ... have failed in Africa, along with everybody else, ...we have not fully understood the problems, and we have not identified the priorities"*.

Washington Post columnist Stephen Rosenfeld put it nicely: *"It is hard to look at black Africa without feeling that something has gone wrong. It is not just the spectacle of suffering that troubles us; it is the sense that we of America and the West who thought we knew how to help these people did not know well enough, although we acted as we did. It is now broadly recognised that our advice has been deeply flawed, not simply among critics but in the establishment circles that provide funds and wield power."*

Djibril Diallo of the U.N. Office put it more bluntly: *"Africa's biggest problem is that too many expatriates are going around the continent with solutions to problems they don't understand. Many of these solutions are half-baked. Not only that, many Africans don't understand African problems"... Africa is dying because it has cut itself in pieces in its ill-planned, ill-advised attempt to "modernise" itself."*

4.6. THE EVIL CONCEPT OF CORRUPTION IN NIGERIA

However, the greatest evil was inflicted on the country by Nigerian leaders themselves. At present, 75% of Nigeria's citizens live on less than US$1 per day, while US$300 billion has disappeared since its independence. Nigeria presents a typical example of how people in a resource-rich country could wallow in abject poverty. The impact of corruption on Nigeria's developmental and governmental processes was manifested in the absence of basic infrastructures, such as schools, roads, hospitals, and many other problems, invariably leading to political instability over 60 years after independence. The most tragic consequence of corruption is its effects on the attitudes and mentality of the people. It has created widespread frustration, disgust, and cynicism, undermining enthusiasm for and faith in the state. Corruption is a systemic issue that has killed Nigeria's private and public sectors, weakened the country and its immunity, and contributed to its stunted development and impoverishment.

Corruption has been a persistent issue in Nigeria for many years, affecting every aspect of society, from the government to business to the everyday lives of its citizens. Bribery, embezzlement, and nepotism are too common in the country, leading to widespread poverty and a lack of trust in government institutions. The country ranks 144 out of 180 on Transparency International's Corruption Perceptions Index, a measure of corruption levels in countries worldwide.

Corruption is like a "hot bitumen that sticks to a madman's cloth, not easily shrugged off but biting and attacking his skin." Corruption is the most neglected human rights violation of our time; it invincibly fuels injustice, inequality, and deprivation and catalyses migration and terrorism in Nigeria. Curbing corruption in Nigeria will not be cured by just changing the government. It is deeply ingrained into the fabric of society, and it requires education about basic economic and regulatory systems, how the economy is run, and ethical values.

In Nigeria, corruption is mostly associated with the bribery of an official person, arguably the most prevalent and costly practice. Nearly everyone in Nigeria has paid a bribe in the past year – some to escape punishment by the police or courts. Still, many are forced to pay for the basic services they desperately need (Transparency International 2015). As a result, most anti-corruption efforts focus on checklists to prevent active (giving) and, to a lesser extent, passive (receiving) bribery. But the reality is that corruption is a very large and complex problem in Nigeria. It shows itself in many public offices as politicians mismanage and divert public funds for their individual and private use, which are supposed to be used for the nation's continental development. The consequences include a strained healthcare system, empty-shell schools, and police protection granted only to the highest bidders. At the same time, the poorest in society are brutalised and left for dead in squalor. Corruption permeates a culture, breeds different practices, inflates costs, hoards products to create artificial scarcity, eliminates competitiveness, reduces the quality of products and services, and discourages foreign and local investment. It destroys credibility, undermines authority, weakens the rule of law, and poisons values, morale, and culture. Corruption cannot be fully solved by legislation or decree. Money laundering from Nigeria to Europe by public officers has been around since Colonial times and has persisted till today.

Causes of Corruption in Nigeria

Bad Governance as a Cause of Corruption. — A government that cheated during an election cannot govern its population correctly, which will encourage corruption at the highest level. Such a government cannot set up and empower monitoring teams to dig deep into private and public establishments' affairs that propagate corruption.

Greed as a Cause of Corruption. — Most corruption centres on greediness, a principal cause of corruption in Nigeria. Many politicians are busy laundering the public funds that should be used for national development into foreign banks instead of solving the unemployment problem.

Poor Accountability. — When those serving in public offices know that they will not be queried or held accountable for how they run their yearly expenses and incomes, there is a possibility that they will indulge in corruption.

Unemployment as a Cause of Corruption in Africa. – An unemployed person is ready to take any action that will fetch them money, whether it involves corrupt practices or not. In offices, people are ready to give bribes to the employer's staff members to secure jobs at the end of an interview.

High Quest for Wealth. — Among the major causes of Corruption in Africa is the high quest for wealth. The government is corrupt, as are the people they rule, and many Africans are ready to give up their lives for money.

4.7 The Concept of the National Cake in Nigeria

A "national cake" mentality is the major affliction that continues to turn politicians into very curious creatures in their bid to force their way into positions of authority. They enter political offices "not intending to serve but to partake of their share of the national cake or to serve those who gave them the platform to achieve more power."

Nigerians coined the phrase "National Cake" in the early 1960s, meaning that every citizen in every corner of the country should partake of the huge economic benefits of crude oil, the "National Cake". This concept has become popular among students, casual workers, commercial drivers, businessmen/women, civil servants, and Nigerian politicians. It links all the national concerns, like principled derivation controversy, state creation controversy, political zoning controversy and incidence of militancy, corruption, kidnapping for ransom, Boko haram, armed robbery, oil theft etc.

Before Nigeria's crude oil era, the country survived on different agricultural products like palm oil, groundnuts, cocoa, etc., with fewer resource-induced problems and conflicts. It was not until 1956 and beyond that Nigeria started experiencing a more pronounced resource-related rift and resentment. The oil boom brought Nigeria onto the global scene.

With oil wealth, Abuja's new capital city was set up at an enviable standard with the construction of several roads and stadia across the country. After a while, the notion of a cake for all was distorted to mean a cake for a few opportunists. Of course, everyone wants to lead because, in the Nigerian context, to lead means to avail oneself of the opportunity to share the national cake. It was seen as a cake without owners. According to the Economist (a British Weekly), "Nigerian leaders are so greedy that they have subverted the entire machinery of the State to serve their needs. The national wealth was ceaselessly shared among a few in power, even on the platform of political parties during meetings and rallies. The more money a Political Party shares, the more members it gets and the more corrupt and powerful it becomes on the country's political scene."

Unfortunately, the ignoble philosophy of national cake has spread from the ruling class to the rest of the populace. This goes a long way to bolster the saying, *"if the head of a fish gets spoiled, the body cannot evade the rot"*. The police officer stops and demands a driver's bribe as his take on the national cake. The receptionist in government offices takes a bribe to progress your file or allow you to see his boss.

4.8 Is Nigeria just a Corrupt Nation or a Cornerstone of Africa?

Nigeria is a complex country with a rich history and diverse culture. On the one hand, Nigeria is known for its rampant corruption, which has long plagued the nation and held back its development. However, it is also often touted as the cornerstone of Africa due to its large economy, abundant natural resources, and vibrant democracy.

Corruption is not unique to Nigeria;it has no monopoly over corruption. Corruption is a problem affecting many countries worldwide. It is a complex issue with deep roots and a wide

range of causes, including a lack of political will, weak institutions, and the influence of powerful special interests, both
internal and external, on the country. Addressing corruption
requires a comprehensive and sustained effort that involves
government action.

Despite these challenges, Nigeria has made some progress in
combating corruption recently. The country has established
anti-corruption bodies and agencies, such as the Economic
and Financial Crimes Commission (EFCC), that have taken action against corrupt officials and business people. In addition,
Nigeria has made some progress in improving transparency in
its government procurement processes and in strengthening
the rule of law.

However, much remains to be done if Nigeria is to overcome
the legacy of corruption and become a truly democratic and
prosperous nation. The country must work to strengthen its
institutions, protect the rights of its citizens, and promote accountability in government. It must also encourage a culture
of transparency and integrity in all aspects of society.

Nigeria has the resources and the potential to overcome corruption and become a thriving, democratic nation. The country has a rich history, a diverse culture, and dynamic, entrepreneurial people. With the right policies and leadership, Nigeria
can harness these strengths to build a brighter future for itself
and Africa.

Solutions to Corruption in Nigeria

A Multistakeholder Approach — A multi-stakeholder approach must be taken for Nigeria to become a genuinely corrupt-free society. The fight against corruption should not only
be waged by the government alone. Civil society, the media,

and the private sector must all play critical roles in holding those in power accountable, promoting transparency and integrity, and fostering a culture of ethical behaviour.

Increase in Education and Awareness of the Negative Impact of Corruption. There is a need for an improvement in education and an increase in the populace's awareness of corruption's negative impact on the economic growth and development of the country, thereby necessitating a change in the cultural and societal norms that enable corruption to thrive.

Self-Satisfaction — Both politicians and Nigerian citizens should be paid a living wage, and they should be satisfied with what they have. They should be satisfied with their monthly salary and not participate in corrupt practices. There will be a reduction in the level of corruption when we all understand that we came into this world with nothing, and with nothing, we will return.

Transparency and Accountability — Corruption is gaining more ground in Nigeria because various departments lack adequate transparency and accountability. Calling up heads of every public and private establishment to give detailed accounts of their spending each year and ensuring that adequate punishment is given to those who abuse their post will make others learn and make amends. That is the practice in China and the South East, and it has minimised corruption.

Establishing a Strong Anti-corruption Group — Setting-up anti-corruption groups in various states should help tackle the challenge posed by unemployment. Also, the group should be independent of the government so that anyone caught in corrupt practice will receive the adequate punishment he deserves.

Employment Creation — Unemployment increases corruption. Creating jobs for citizens will go a long way to minimising the country's involvement in dirty businesses like drug and human trafficking.

Multinational Corporations and Companies also have a role to play in the fight against corruption in Nigeria. On the one hand, these companies can bring much-needed investment, technology, and jobs to the country, which can help to promote economic growth and development. On the other hand, they should avoid following bad practices that encourage corruption.

Firstly, multinational corporations must avoid corrupt practices such as bribery and embezzlement to secure business advantages or win contracts in Nigeria. This undermines the integrity of the business sector and erodes public trust in the government and the private sector.

Secondly, multinational corporations should stop engaging in tax evasion and avoidance, which deprives the Nigerian government of much-needed revenue and reduces the resources available to the government to address poverty and inequality and to invest in education, health, and infrastructure.

Thirdly, multinational corporations should stop exploiting the weak regulations and lax enforcement of anti-corruption laws, which allows them to operate with little accountability. This creates an uneven playing field that advantages multinational corporations over local businesses, which can undermine local entrepreneurship and reduce economic growth.

In addition, multinational corporations can also engage in partnerships with civil society organisations and other stakeholders to promote transparency, accountability, and good governance. This can include supporting anti-corruption initiatives, participating in transparency and accountability initiatives, and collaborating with local communities to address corruption.

The International Community can also play a role by promoting greater corporate responsibility and supporting anti-corruption initiatives in Nigeria. This can be achieved through technical assistance, sharing of best practices, and providing funding for anti-corruption initiatives. The international community can also help by providing trade and investment opportunities and promoting greater regional integration, which can help create an environment where corruption is less likely to thrive.

In conclusion, Nigeria has a complex corruption legacy but also a rich growth and development potential. While corruption remains a major challenge, there is reason to be hopeful about the country's future. The fight against corruption in Nigeria is a long-term, complex effort that requires a sustained and multi-stakeholder approach. While the challenges are many, the potential benefits of a corrupt-free Nigeria are enormous. With the right policies, leadership, and engagement from all sectors of society, Nigeria can overcome corruption and realise its full potential as a cornerstone of Africa and a beacon of hope for the world.

4.9 The Exorbitant Cost of Governance

Nigeria has one of the highest costs of running the government. This section was extracted from an article written by Ifeanyi Nanocurie 2015.

The 1999 Constitution recognises the Nigerian government as a Federal System of government. It further stipulates that there are three main tiers of government – Executive, Legislature, and Judiciary – who must be independent of one another.

This has led to layers upon sub-layers of government branches that take up a big chunk of the government revenue.

Federal Executive

- **Ministry:** Nigeria has over 26 ministries with a Minister and permanent secretaries heading each ministry. An example of a Ministry is the Ministry of Health.

- **Department:** A department is headed by a Director (and deputy)

- **Agency:** Federal Executive bodies perform various functions, e. g. National Agency for Food and Drug Administration and Control (NAFDAC).

- **Commissions:** Commissions perform the same forms as departments and agencies. E. g. Economic and Financial Crimes Commission (EFCC).

- **Security**, e. g. the Nigerian Army, Police and Navy.

The heads and deputies of these federal branches earn over N1 Million ($2,000) monthly, along with official cars, houses, allowances, salaries, pensions, and others.

The Federal Government of Nigeria is the largest employer in the country.

State Executive — Like the Federal Executive, the State Executive has its ministries headed by Commissioners and permanent secretaries who earn at least N1 million ($2,000) in salaries, gratuities and pensions. In Nigeria, states depend solely on allocations from the Federal Government to pay salaries.

Local Government — The official 776 Local Government Areas in Nigeria have Chairmen and Chairpersons voted into office, and they, too, have lots of staff who earn salaries and allowances.

The Judiciary has Federal courts of appeal, state courts of appeal, Magistrate Courts, and others. The highest court in the land is the Supreme Court of Nigeria.

The Legislature has a federal legislature making up the Senate (Upper Chamber) with 109 members and the House of Representatives (Lower Chamber) with 360 members. There are 776 Honourables across Nigeria at the state level, representing the 776 Local Government Area's in Nigeria.

A Nigerian senator earns over N29 million ($70,000) per annum, and the national minimum rate is N360,000 ($862). In comparison, his American counterpart earns $174,000 per annum while the national minimum rate is $15,080.

The former Governor of the Central Bank, Sanusi Lamido Sanusi, said in 2013 that the Nigerian legislature takes 20% of the Nigerian annual budget. The costs of maintaining our legislative branch at the federal and state levels are high, contributing to Nigeria's governance cost.

President Goodluck Jonathan said in 2013 that 70% of Nigerian earnings are spent on recurrent expenditure, and over 52% are used in paying salaries, pensions and gratuities. This is rather bad for a developing country like Nigeria, where over 70% of the population is poor. Regrettably, the system is fashioned in a way that doesn't allow for capital project development but provides for excessive spending of taxpayers' money to maintain the luxury of government officials. A government that wants to cater to its people shouldn't be running on such huge costs.

With the level of underdevelopment and insecurity in the country, Nigeria needs to cut down the salaries of all lawmakers and executive members. There is also the need to merge areas where functions are duplicated to save money. Suppose that Senegal's Senate President could approve the scrapping of that country's Senate, save money for his country, and pump the recovered money (excess allowance and salaries) into meaningful ventures and projects. Nigeria should see this as a good model and do the same.

5. How other Africans perceive Nigerian

As a member of the Nigerian diaspora, I have had the opportunity to meet many other Africans than I would not have met if I were in Nigeria. Also, as someone who trained farmers across Africa, I was often easily spotted as Nigerian by my accent but sometimes confused as a Ghanaian by my demeanour and lackadaisical attitude.

As the most populous country in Africa with a vibrant cultural scene and one of the largest economies on the continent, Nigeria is often viewed as a bellwether or leader for African politics and society.

On the one hand, Nigerians are often seen as outgoing and friendly people with great national pride and are admired for their entrepreneurial spirit and cultural contributions to the continent. On the other hand, Nigerians are sometimes perceived as arrogant and overly ambitious and have a tendency to dominate and intimidate others.

Additionally, many Nigerians (approximately 5 million) living and working in other African countries have sometimes led to tensions and conflicts, with some accusing Nigerians of taking jobs and resources away from locals.

Undoubtedly, the mixed perception of Nigerians by other Africans is a complex and nuanced issue. But it is also important for Nigerians to be aware of how other Africans perceive them and to work towards building positive relationships and strengthening ties with other countries on the continent. And non-Nigeria needs to understand the drive and aspirations of Nigerians better.

This section uses some feedback from Quoras.com members and qualitative feedback from the sample of non-Nigerians interviewed in the United Kingdom.

Here is a comment from an anonymous non-Nigerian:

"Africans, in general, are tranquil, laidback and religious people. They believe in helping their poor family members and see riches not as an end goal but rather as a by-product of God's blessings of one's deeds. As a result, many ordinary Africans do not earnestly seek riches as in Western countries, but Nigerians are an exception to this laid-back approach to life". He continued, "Many Nigerians are so money conscious they are loud, aggressive, cocky and arrogant and will do anything to make it in life either by fair or foul means. In their quest to make it, they mistake other Africans' laid-back approach for laziness or not being as smart as they are.

Many times when other Africans are living with Nigerians overseas, we get angry about their behaviour because citizens of many Western countries already have a stereotype of Africans as a bunch of people who are "scams", loud, and corrupt. Africans from other countries often try their best to follow the law and refrain from loud and criminal behaviour to prove our hosts wrong and disabuse them of the false notion that Africans are loud, corrupt and not law-abiding.

This is the reason why it appears many Africans hate Nigerians. In conclusion, other Africans do not hate Nigerians. Instead, we "love the sinners and hate the sin".

This statement about Nigerians is very profound, and it is worth looking at closely. The first is to examine what's behind the Nigerians''s drive to succeed.

As was mentioned earlier, Nigeria is the most populous country in Africa, with a population of over 200 million people and the seventh most populous country in the world. In addition, the country is also a melting pot of cultures and traditions. Its diverse population has over 500 ethnic groups and over 1000 languages spoken. Nigeria is characterised by intense ethnic polarization, conflict, and competition. The heavy competitive nature amongst the different ethnic entities in Nigeria creates this natural competitive nature of Nigerians in the diaspora.

For most Nigerians, a competitive drive to succeed in all circumstances is deeply entrenched in their psyche. Even walking through Lagos, Onitsha or Abuja's buzzing market, you will inevitably encounter smart buyers striving to snag the best prices by attempting to negotiate with traders in their languages.

A Cameroonian narrated his first experience in Nigeria. He landed at Lagos airport early morning (4 am). On his way to the city, looking through the window, he noticed people (in their thousands) alongside the highway. He could not understand why so many people were outside and walking about so early in the morning. Suddenly his vehicle stopped because of the traffic. The vehicle was swarmed by more than twenty hawkers offering to sell all sorts of things, from chewing gums and bread to sausage and cigarettes. At first, he was terrified and felt the vehicle was about to be attacked and robbed. There were only two of them in the vehicle. After realising he was not in danger, he was shocked by the volume of people pushing each other and trying to sell to only two people and asked himself, "how much do they even make per day selling these things? There is so much competition everywhere. It then dawned on him that no matter how much or little they were making, they had to be up early and be passionate if they wanted to make any money. Most Nigerians have that kind of "survival of the fittest" mentality.

Someone once described a Nigerian inner city as a typical African jungle, "*Every morning in Africa, a gazelle wakes up, it knows it must outrun the fastest lion, or it will be killed. Every morning in Africa, a lion wakes up and knows it must run faster than the slowest gazelle, or it will starve to death. It doesn't matter whether you're a lion or a gazelle when the sun rises; you'd better be running.*"

This African saying reflects literarily how Nigerian are trained to perceive life. High expectations are expected from Nigerian children from an early age. Nigerian culture has an inherent element that children must do better than their parents in every way. As a result, Nigerians grow up to become highly ambitious people with an insatiable appetite for success because everyone knows that no one is safe or immune to the vicissitudes of life that successful and not-so-successful people encounter. Nigerian children are trained from childhood that when the sun comes up, you'd better start struggling to succeed until your good become better and your better become best. It is imbibed in every Nigerian that you need to develop a progressive and possibility-oriented mindset that will motivate you to pursue your goals and achieve your dreams, or else you will lose out and perish.

This drive is often recognised and sometimes appreciated by many non-Nigerian Africans. For example:

BD — *I'm South African and used to stay in Sunnyside Pretoria, aka Lagos of South Africa. I have a good number of wonderful friends, colleagues and acquaintances from West Africa that I met* *during my university days and now professionally as colleagues and clients. Those people I know socially, and I can safely say my former neighbours were 50% Nigerians. My view of Nigerians are the following, in no particular order:*

They are well-spoken: yes, there's pidgin, but most Nigerians are eloquent and expressive, sometimes a bit over-the-top; they are quite industrious: but can also be cut-throat and unethical in business.

Nigerians are well-travelled and will explore any avenue to make money elsewhere, which is wonderful. But I think it's partially because of their adventurous and get-it spirit coupled with the fact that millions of Nigerians are desperate to leave Nigeria for a better life elsewhere.

I love Nigerian music. I listen to a mix of Asa, Mr Eazi with the delicious lips, Timaya, Harry Songs, Runtown, who just so fine, a few Davido tracks, love Tiwa and Wizkid;

Nigerians have their many tribal prejudices and discriminatory attitudes but will come together against an outsider. I like the accent, Nollywood; the plot, twist, and magic. ......"

I G Kenya – "*Nigerians are focused on what they do, hardworking and have confidence even when they are not sure. They are spiritual, either Godly or ungodly/witchcraft. Nigerians have issues, but when a third party steps in, they quickly unite and fight the intruder. After that, they go back to their differences. Therefore, they love their own. That's why when two of them are new in a place, give it time, and you will see 10 of them. A real copy of Indian/ Asian. They like enjoying life to the fullest They are experts in conning in all manners — I think they studied their Colonial masters very well. They are like Kikuyu in Kenya — if you mind your business, they won't bother you. Additionally, they are excellent either in education or business. Most of them are good academics.*"

Annestecia — "As a *Cameroonian, I grew up watching Nigerian movies* and hearing stories from Cameroonian traders who work in Nigeria. I always see Nigerians as a country with the most business-minded people, and they will go to any extent to make money. While many are true believers, some are fake, ritualists and scammers. But my visit and interaction with Nigerians in 2014, 2019 and 2020 changed my perception. They are so welcoming; their hospitality towards me was beyond my imagination. Nevertheless, when in Nigeria, be smart. Nigerians are considered very smart, but some are famous for using that smartness to do unglamorous activities."

DB Kenya – "*Nigeria is a country with many people... the largest population in Africa ...... You get to hear lots of opinions about them, such as they are con artists and deceitful. But my personal opinion is that for a huge society, you expect to have all kinds of characters. As an East African...specifically Kenyan, I find their culture and way of life interesting, and I want to get to know it. Being Bantu, I can relate to and understand most east and southern African tribes, but western Africa is quite different.*"

SV – Ghanian – "*I have spent a lot of time around Nigerians. Judging from the ones I've met, this is my opinion. Nigerians are very entrepreneurial. Of all the west African states, it's no surprise that Nigerians have built the largest and most successful indigenous companies.*

Nigerians are very serious about education. Almost all of the Nigerians that I know are college educated, and many have multiple degrees. Nigerians are confident and can accomplish anything, and some will confidently tell you this. Nigerians are very intelligent and love to debate. Despite all their country's challenges, Nigerians love their country, and most see a positive future for Nigeria".

Nigeria is considered a collectivist society and individuals pursuing success are committed to the well-being, pride and prosperity of the family or tribe. As a result, parents push their children and drive them to achieve, and the children are indoctrinated with this cultural belief. Almost every parent aspires to send their children to the best school. Even Nigeria's national anthem reminds children to strive to attain *"great lofty heights"* and sternly reminds us that *"the labour of our heroes past shall never be in vain."*

Nigerians' entrepreneurial, resourceful and "can-do" attitude enable them to find innovative solutions to their challenges. This spirit of entrepreneurship is reflected in the thriving informal sector of the economy that operates without government help, which employs a significant proportion (60%) of the country's population. This entrepreneurial spirit gives Nigerians hope for the future, as they believe they can create a better life for themselves and their families—Nigerians' drive to succeed springs from hardship. Most of the successful Nigerian entrepreneurial people in the world are those who understand infrastructural precarity.

Nigerians are also known to congregate with one another when they migrate abroad. This has served as a support system for their people, especially new immigrants trying to find their bearing. Nigerians especially assemble according to their tribes and ethnic groups and host periodic meetings and events to build communal relationships.

Nigerians hold education in high regard because it has proven to be the country's consistent leveller and equalizer. Many have risen from the gutters to prestigious statuses due to the education they acquired, so people prioritize education even when they migrate to other countries. As early as primary school, students are ranked first to last for each subject at the end of each school year. Children are expected to amass multiple degrees, get a good job and earn enough to care for their parents in old age. In addition, they are subtly warned to avoid "non-traditional" careers such as arts and literature and to focus on respectable vocations such as a doctor, barrister or engineer. Currently, over 190,000 new Nigerian Students study abroad a year, with a substantial amount going to the UK and the USA.

TM South Africa – "*Their level of intelligence amazes me, I love how passionate they are about education, and that is one thing I admire about Nigerians. The fact that they are so intelligent blows my mind every time. I like having conversations with them because I know I will learn something.*

They have this aura around them that is always positive and they have a lot of energy and like to party. I found it very uncomfortable when I first encountered outspoken Nigerians, but now I laugh it off.

When it comes to the issue of them being scammers, drug dealers etc. I have mixed emotions about that because I feel every country has good and bad eggs, so wrapping everyone with the same cloth would be unfair as good Nigerians excel in great things in other countries worldwide. It has nothing to do with criminal activities, and if you hang around with them, you are bound to have a good time.

Overall I think they are passionate people, outspoken (one of the things I really love about them), and they are proud Africans, LOL, I have met a lot of African people in South Africa, and I can tell you there is no pride like Nigerian Pride".

FA – Togolese "*Nigerians are practically my brethren. In short, Nigerians are among the most amicable, friendly, genuine, and fun people one could meet and spend time with. I think they're* *so friendly and open that a foreigner who's never been to Nigeria may find it weird."*

YA Kenya — *"I've concluded that Nigeria is the greatest country in Africa, whether we like it or not. Nigeria is the greatest country in Africa. These people have great music, food, and fashion, and they've mastered the most important thing, being themselves. You can spot a Nigerian from a mile away. They don't try to copy how other people do their thing. They don't try to get an accent if they're living abroad. And Nigerian was born a Nigerian, and they will die Nigerian, me being African and me being Kenyan. It's hard for me to admit this, but it's the truth...... So, for anybody going abroad, I tell you this: make some Nigerian friends; these people are gangsters. Let me tell you, they know the law. They know the ins and outs of countries, and if you go to a country as a black man and there's no Nigerian ran away, there's nothing good there. ..... these people are so flamboyant and so loud in their lifestyle that they don't care where they are, even if they in Europe, or America; Nigerians, just a Nigerian man wishes to be a Nigerian."*

Nancy Cameroon – *"I have observed that Nigeria as a whole is blessed and that whatever Nigerians set their hands to do prospers (good or bad). I sometimes refer to Nigeria as the land of the good, the bad, and the rotten. When you come across the good ones, they're good people indeed, but when you come across the ones with the ugly character, you wouldn't even know until it is too late. I love their confidence and they don't give a shit what others think about them, whether you perceive them as loud, dubious, tribalistic or whatever. They won't change who they are to make you happy. Again, I am flabbergasted at their confidence in both good and bad things, and they can be very domineering. They won't embrace another man's culture easily, but you must embrace theirs."*

Nigerians are hardworking and resilient, especially abroad, with a strong desire to succeed, fuelled by a lack of opportunities at home and unpleasant situations. They are motivated and encouraged to strive hard and excel because returning home empty-handed is not an option. A 2018 report on the integration of migrants in the German labour market, issued by the Institute for Employment Agency, shows that Nigerians have an edge in finding jobs in Germany. This has been be attributed to the fact that Nigerians are hardworking, dedicated, and committed in their workplace.

AD Central African Republic – *"Nigerian are strong in everything, strong in population, strong in movies, strong in selling bullshits, strong in music, strong in criminality, strong in science and strong in scams. Well, Nigeria is like the other African countries multiplied by ten."*

AA Uganda — *"When I was told while working in East Africa that my next assignment would take me to Nigeria, I immediately began asking my African colleagues what they thought of Nigeria.*

The first words from many of them — primarily Ugandans, Kenyans and Congolese — whether they had any experience with Nigeria or Nigerians or not — were something similar to Nigerian craftiness, sometimes in the sharp, shrewd sense. But more often than not, in the sense of the devious, guileful and sly. Then maybe there would be the talk of Nigerian culture, music, movies and their peculiar English. This may be an unfair shake, but that was the impression East Africans gave me of Nigerians before arriving in Nigeria."

CG Ghanian – *"I firmly believe Nigeria is truly the pulse of Africa — they shape popular culture and have a strong economy. Nigerians have a strong sense of pride which comes off as arrogant at times — most Africans should aspire to their level of pride. Nearly* *all of my black friends in college and medical school were Nigerians. They are very driven and educated."*

In addition, many Nigerian students that could not travel out of the country had to endure studying with a poor quality basic infrastructure, such as limited power and water supply, bad roads and poor telecommunications systems, a lack which sometimes undermines and cripples their academic achievements. It is easier to see why these students have high academic achievements and records when they are in developed countries with better facilities. For instance, in 2017, Christiana Esio Udoh, 26 years, a Ph. D. student of Chemical Engineering at the British imperial college, won the prestigious and desirable Dudley Newitt Prize for experimental excellence. In 2019, 46 Nigerian of the 96 medical students recorded an astounding feat of success at Howard University, USA. Of the 27 awards of excellence given at the prestigious institution's graduation ceremony, 16 were claimed by Nigerian graduates. Victory Yinka-Banjo, a 17-year-old high school graduate, was offered more than 5 million dollars of scholarship money for an undergraduate program of study.

SV Zimbabwe – *"Almost all of the Nigerians I know are college educated and have multiple degrees. Nigerians are confident, and nothing stops them from accomplishing their goals; some will confidently tell you this. Nigerians are very intelligent and love to debate. Despite all of its issues, Nigerians love their country, and most see a positive future for Nigeria".*

MA Ghanians — *"I am a Ghanaian, and I see Nigerians as hardworking, entrepreneurial, and creative, evidenced in their movie industries and business ventures. They make 'survival struggles' better as hustlers in Ghana than most Ghanaians."*

However, this dominance was often viewed negatively as a source of pride by many non-Nigerians. It can also lead to resentment among other African nations who felt Nigeria was imposing its will on the rest of the continent.

MD – Zambia – *"I am originally Zambian, and Zambians just as much dislike Nigerians as many citizens of Southern Africa. From a Southern African perspective, I think it's a cultural difference-oriented dislike, and most Nigerians' behaviours are opposite to what we consider normal behaviour.*

Secondly, Nigerians are hard-working. Do we dislike them for being hard-working? No. We dislike how some may go to any length to achieve something. ... A few, not all Nigerians, are flat out into illegal activities like drugs. Sadly, they make people believe this is Nigerians' general way of life."

NB – South Africa *"No, we do not hate Nigeria or Nigerians. Nigerians are our African pride; imagine Africa or the world without Nigeria, and Africa would have been bullied worldwide. We compete in certain spaces with Nigeria generally for bragging rights, if for anything, and ARE Nigerians proud of their success! I am South African and I think Nigerians don't own any oligopoly of any organized crime from harvesting, refining, and distribution to retail. Be it cigarettes, diamonds, oil, or cyber. And for a country with more than 200 million people, speaking hundreds of different languages, you are bound to bump into one negatively in the diaspora."*

Anonymous South Africa *"Suppose you looked at Wall Street's top 100 investment bankers today. In that case, you'd find a healthy percentage of them are Nigerians, the top brain surgeons in the world today healthy percentage of them Nigerians, the top investment banking lawyers in the world today the healthy percentage of the Nigerians. What does that tell you? ....? And then you look at where you'll find those Nigerians, and typically, it's not in Nigeria. .....So I want to say this to all South Africans. If you want to destroy the economy. Let the Nigerian talent leave*

BA Ghana — *"As a Ghanaian, I can tell you that things are tense right now concerning Ghana-Nigeria relations resulting from the uptick in kidnappings + ransom in Ghana, which was a crime that was more or less non-existent in the mainstream. This has erupted paranoia about the number of Nigerians in Ghana, how many of them are engaged in petty trading (which is illegal and disrupting the local market share) and how they are (allegedly) increasing crime."*

AQ East Africa – *"For many — maybe most — of us in East Africa, Nigeria is a somewhat uncouth, made-up place, a mix of arguing communities with inept leadership. The place has resources and money, but only a few thousand people benefit from it. It's a dog-eat-dog sort of place, with millions of would-be con artists without the wit to do it right. Bling, padded shoulders, swanky dress, and the rich rubbing the ordinary people's noses in their poverty. We think of it as our older, jock brother, who married a hooker and tried to persuade the rest of us she's actually the brothel owner. We just shake our heads for Nigerians."*

GNOA Ghanaians – *"Ghanians do not hate Nigerians and Nigerians do not hate Ghanaians! The two countries are anglophone neighbours in a largely francophone West African region. Economically, many foreign investors see Ghana, with its 25 million population as essentially a part of Nigeria with its population of 200 million and the biggest economy in all of Africa. This is rather like the relationship between the US and Canada or the UK and the Republic of Ireland. The economy of Lagos — between 15 and 20 million people — is bigger than the economy of all of Ghana. Ghanaians get irritated by what they see as pushy Nigerians who see and describe their country as their "little neighbour ", and Ca-*

nadians often feel the same about their US neighbours. But — and get this — ask any Ghanaian which African nation's citizens they feel closest to, without exception, they will almost always say Nigerians. Ask any Nigerian the same question and the answer will nearly always be Ghanaians!"

JD Zimbabwe — *"They disregard other nationalities and Nigerians are too biased towards their fellow Nigerians. It is a strong streak of patriotism; they easily unite towards a common goal or enemy but when they are among themselves, they fight each other, hindering progress and change".*

PA Zimbabwe — *"Most Nigerians I have met are very friendly, and it is easy to start a conversation, typically about business, fashion or politics. Some Nigerian women always talk negatively about their Nigerian counterparts. I always get the usual from females when they realisethat I am married to a Nigerian: "Why do South African women like our men?" Be careful. They want your documents but are married back home."*

MD – Zambia — *"These guys can be annoyingly loud for no reason to be, and a conversation with them sounds like an argument or a fight. We detest this about them."*

It is a common stereotype that Nigerians are louder than other Africans. However, this stereotype can be attributed to several factors. First is the population of Nigeria, with 200 million people representing one in every five black people in Africa. Its cultural trends and communication styles may be more visible and influential than other African countries. Also, Nigerian cultural norms and communication styles mean if you want to be heard, you need to speak direct and assertively, which can be perceived as loud or even confrontational by those not used to it. Nigerians are often highly expressive and passionate in their intense communication, and raising their voice can also come across as loud. Picture a home in Nigeria; unlike in the UK, where the average family is four people, many Nigerian homes are larger, as many as ten, with lots of people passionately gisting and the background noise of the generator for local electricity. If you whisper in this environment, nobody will hear you; you have to raise your voice to be heard.

While cultural, environmental and historical factors may have contributed to these perceptions, it is also important to recognize that different communication styles and cultural norms should be respected and valued rather than judged or stereotyped.

Feedback about Nigeria from other non-African countries

William English – *"In my short time working with Nigerians, I have found that they are hardworking and always looking to learn more. This hunger for knowledge is unmatched. I can remember sitting down next to a man who was almost the same age as my grandad, and he was doing a university course. I wish the U.K. youth could be so motivated to study".*

M Polish — *"Throughout the years, I have worked with people from Nigeria. I found them very helpful, and they had a good sense of humour and enthusiasm and were grateful and appreciative.*

When you get to know them, they are very loyal and stand together no matter what. They are like family to each other, sharing food and very giving towards others. They are very protective of each other. If everyone could be like this to one another, this world would a better place to coexist."

K English — *"They are always happy, bubbly and friendly. They treat you as one big family and support you when you are in need. The way they interact with you."*

5.1. THE IMPACT OF DIVERSITY ON NIGERIAN CULTURE

Before meeting the Europeans, Nigeria had over 500 languages, over 1000 dialects, and ethnic groups. The English language in Nigeria started with the advent of British explorers in the nineteenth century. It led to the passage of the Education Ordinance Act of 1926, which gave prominence to the proper use of English. It made an English certification a prerequisite for employment in most professions in Nigeria.

By default, all Nigerians are bilingual, but many can speak more than three languages. The ability to speak English and two or more languages gave Nigeria some advantage. Charlemagne once said, "*to speak another language is to hold a second soul in your possession.*" Multilingualism is the ability to speak more than two different languages fluently. This ability allows the speaker to perceive the world differently. Each language allows the individual to access a culture with a different take on an idea under debate. Even walking through Lagos, Onitsha or Abuja's buzzing markets, you will inevitably encounter multilingual smart sellers. For these vendors, multilingualism is a unique selling proposition that allows them to sell their goods to many buyers.

Chomsky argues that the language faculty in the human brain enables a child to learn any language in about four years. Most Nigerian youth in the inner city are born into situations where they must learn multiple languages in their youth because that is the only way to function in a multilingual and multi-ethnic society successfully. Whereas those born in rural areas may afford to be bilingualism (with some form of English or Arabic), however, they must learn more languages if they are going to survive in the city.

A study shows that it takes the average person about six months to develop fluency in a different language with daily studies. However, once you successfully learn your first language to become bilingual, it is much easier to become multilingual. That is why most Nigerians find it easy to learn another language and settle in the countries they find themselves in (e.g. French, Mandarin or German).

The ability of Nigerian to learn and speak multiple languages increases their adaptability and employment chances exponentially. Studies also show that an employee can earn up to 15% more by learning one new language. Fluency in new languages also makes studying overseas and conversing with different community groups possible and allows one to celebrate the diversity in human cultures instead of being scared of them.

Studies have shown that people with multiple languages are more confident and have a better sense of knowing where they fit in their different societies. They also experience lower levels of fear and anxiety and are less likely to experience a mental health disorder, cognitive decline or a stroke. Nigeria's diverse language and culture may have contributed to students' intelligence and working memory and influenced the students' ability to perform academically.

Another factor is the Anglocentric inclination of Nigerian families. Every family, including semi-literate ones, wants to expose their children to the English language right from the early stages of childhood to increase their "social belongingness." Colonisation has taught Nigerians that individual intelligence could be measured by the ability to speak the Queen's English.

Below is an anonymous quote. It reads, "*The British both colonised Nigeria and India. But India rejected the British religion and culture, food, and the British way of doing things but held unto British technology, while the Nigerians accepted the British culture, dress code, food and religion but rejected the British technology. That is why the Indians are currently more advanced in technology; they don't need to speak English to make a cell phone. However, Nigerians are colonised to believe that the more we speak better English, the more intelligent we are. But the truth is that perfect English is not a mark of intelligence; it is a mark of linguistics".*

Nigeria has the potential to become a model for other countries in the region and the world, demonstrating that a country rich in resources and cultural diversity can overcome challenges and achieve its full potential. The government must prioritize education to meet the country's technological and developmental needs, further the well-being of its citizens, and work towards economic and social development that benefits all Nigerians.

Education is their best weapon against impoverishment, disease, early marriage, gang activities, and prostitution. Educated children stand a better chance of having opportunities for constructive and positive life paths. However, it is critical to promote an education system that is "fit for purpose" with a strong focus on entrepreneurship and technology to optimise opportunities. The potential for Nigeria to leverage its human capital lies in its ability to invest in the education and training of children and young people. Investments in education will lead to a qualified and employable workforce that meets the demands of the labour markets for skills and competencies.

5.2. **NIGERIAN TIMEKEEPING**

Nigerian time (or African time) is the perceived cultural tendency of Nigerians toward a more relaxed attitude to time. This usually expresses Nigerian tardiness in appointments, meetings and events. This also includes the more leisurely, relaxed, and less rigorously scheduled lifestyle found in many African countries, especially as opposed to the more clock-bound pace of daily life in Western countries.

However, Nigeria's lax attitude towards time reflects a different approach and method in managing tasks, events, and interactions. For example, a Nigerian tends to have more "emotional time consciousness" , which contrasts with Western "mechanical time consciousness".

The reality is that this lax attitude to time was typical in all agrarian societies before the middle of the eighteenth century — the beginning of the Industrial Revolution. Prior to this period, the natural rhythms of the days and the seasons were sufficient for the farmer, and all times were local.

From the late seventeenth century, the accuracy of the time mechanisms gradually improved because coordination was essential to bring supplies of raw materials together, organise workers and distribute their output. Factories demanded all the workers arrive simultaneously to run the machines and start production. Workers were also made to work per hour to improve their productivity and deliver the order on time.

Nigerian time has become a key topic of self-criticism. Some believe that one of the main reasons for the continuing underdevelopment of Nigeria is the carefree attitude to time and the need for punctuality in all aspects of life.

6. What the World can Learn from Nigeria

The Nigerian state is one of the most ethnically diverse societies in the world. Nigeria is not only a multi-ethnic entity, it is also multi-lingual, multi-religious, and multi-cultural.

The country has over 500 languages and over 1000 dialects and ethnic groups. The four largest ethnic groups are the Hausa and Fulani, who are predominant in the north; the Igbo, who are predominant in the southeast; and the Yoruba, who are predominant in the southwest. The rest of Nigeria's ethnic groups (sometimes called 'minorities') are found nationwide. The Fulani and the Hausa are also predominantly Muslim, while the Igbo, Efik, Ibibio, and Annang people are mainly Christian. The Yoruba have a balance of members adherent to Islam and Christianity. Indigenous religions, such as worshipping ancestral spirits and using traditional medicine known as "juju" remain important in Nigeria's ethnic groups, from the Egungun Festival, which is a celebration of ancestral spirits, to the Calabar Carnival. Nigeria's festivals and celebrations are a true representation of the country's rich cultural heritage. This blend of religious beliefs has resulted in Nigeria's vibrant and diverse spiritual landscape. Nigeria is famous for its English language literature. Apart from the 'pure' English-speaking population, Nigerian pidgin is also a common lingua franca. Roughly a third of Nigeria's population speaks Pidgin English, a simplified language form which uses a primary English lexicon. For instance, "How you dey" would be substituted for "How are you".

Nigerian cuisine is also a reflection of the country's diverse cultural heritage. It celebrates flavour and diversity with various fresh and flavourful dishes. Some popular dishes include jollof rice, pounded yam, egusi soup, and suya, a grilled meat dish popular in many West African countries.

Jollof rice   Suya meat. *www.thecable.ng/*

Nigeria's cultural complexity and diversity are a testament to the country's rich history and traditions. Nigeria's culture celebrates diversity and reflects its vibrant and colourful heritage with a rich blend of indigenous practices, religious beliefs, artistic expressions, cuisine, and festivals.

6.1. LESSONS FROM THE COMPLEXITY AND DIVERSITY OF NIGERIA'S CULTURE

The complexity and diversity of Nigerian culture are a source of inspiration for the rest of the world. With its rich blend of indigenous practices, religious beliefs, artistic expressions, cuisine, and festivals, Nigeria's culture offers valuable lessons that can help foster a more harmonious and inclusive world.

Cultural diversity — Nigeria's cultural diversity should inspire the world to embrace a more inclusive and accepting approach towards different cultures and ways of life. Nigeria's rich mix of indigenous practices, religious beliefs, and artistic expressions provides a clear example of how different cultures can coexist and interact positively and harmoniously. Instead of viewing cultural differences as a source of division, Nigerians have been able to use their cultural diversity to create a vibrant and dynamic society. This is evident in how different cultural expressions blend to create unique and innovative music, dance, and cuisine forms. The world can work towards creating more inclusive communities where different cultures are valued, respected, and celebrated rather than divided.

Cultural tolerance and respect. Despite the differences in language, religion, and customs, Nigerians have a long history of peaceful coexistence and mutual respect. This is evident in how different ethnic groups celebrate each other's festivals, embrace each other's religious beliefs, and embrace each other's traditions. The world can learn to be more tolerant and respectful of cultural differences.

Preserving and promoting cultural heritage. Despite the challenges posed by modernization and globalization, Nigeria has managed to preserve its cultural heritage and promote its rich artistic expressions, including music, dance, and visual arts. This not only preserves the country's cultural heritage but also helps to pass it down to future generations. The world can strive to preserve its own cultural heritage and promote its artistic expressions to preserve its unique cultural identity.

Nigerians are optimistic – Nigeria, the most populous country in Africa, has a unique cultural identity that is reflected in its people's spirit of optimism. If you live in Nigeria, it will be easy for you to understand why having a sense of optimism is vital to survival in the future. Despite the numerous challenges faced by the country, such as political instability, corruption, economic hardships, and social unrest, Nigerians continue to exhibit a resilient and hopeful attitude towards the future.

The evidence of an optimistic spirit lies everywhere in Nigeria. On the way, they hustle and talk. Nigerian rarely say negative things to themselves at all. When a Nigerian tells you ''I will become the greatest by force,'' please understand he is not bragging. He is speaking his dreams into existence. There is no room for despair. For all its political and economic troubles, Nigerians remain optimistic and happy.

Nigerians are inherently resilient. They have a strong sense of community and can band together to overcome challenges. This resilience was born from the country's turbulent history, including the civil war, the various military coups and the economic challenges. Nigerians have learned to adapt and survive in the face of adversity, creating a culture of resilience that is deeply ingrained in the Nigerian psyche. When your culture is preternaturally positive despite often brutal political, health and social conditions, optimism drives and inspires you to expect success in almost any circumstance. This drive is reflected in the thriving informal sector of the economy, which employs a significant proportion of the country's population. This optimistic spirit gives Nigerians hope for the future, as they believe they can create a better life for themselves and their families.

Nigerians are deeply religious. The country is evenly split between Christians and Muslims, and both religions are practised with great devotion. Religion is significant in Nigerians' lives and provides comfort and hope in difficult times. The strong belief in a higher power in control of the future gives Nigerians the strength to face the challenges that life throws their way. This religious attitude is visible in common Nigerian names: Blessing, Testimony, Mercy, Godspeed and Goodluck – the name of one of the former presidents. In 2011, Nigeria was crowned the most optimistic nation in the world for the second straight year and believed that no matter the hardship, "no condition is permanent,". Many Nigerians grew up believing that opportunities don't come knocking on the doors, but rather, we chase them, knowing God is always on our side. In Nigeria, there is a saying, "you aspire to acquire, so that what you admire and desire will not expire but give way for you to inspire others."

In conclusion, the complexity and diversity of Nigerian culture offer valuable lessons for the rest of the world. By embracing cultural tolerance and respect, preserving cultural heritage, and viewing cultural differences as a source of strength and unity, the world can learn from Nigeria's cultural diversity and work towards a more harmonious and inclusive world.

6.2. LESSONS THAT THE WORLD CAN LEARN FROM THE BIAFRA WAR IN NIGERIA

The Biafra War, also known as the Nigerian Civil War, was a devastating conflict that lasted from 1967 to 1970 and resulted in an estimated 13 million deaths. Although the conflict was primarily a struggle for secession by the Igbo people in south-eastern Nigeria, it has important lessons for the world.

The danger of ethnic and religious divisions in society — Nigeria is a diverse country with over 500 ethnic groups, and the conflict was fuelled partly by tensions between the Igbo and other groups. The violence and suffering resulting from the conflict demonstrate the importance of promoting unity and understanding between different social groups.

The importance of democracy and the peaceful resolution of conflicts — A military coup and subsequent counter-coup sparked the war. The government's failure to address the secessionist movement's grievances led to a devastating conflict. This underscores the importance of building strong democratic institutions and ensuring citizens have a voice in their government.

The war highlights the devastating impact of hunger and famine on civilian populations. The blockade of Biafra by the Nigerian government, which prevented food and medical supplies from reaching the region, led to the deaths of hundreds of thousands of civilians. This serves as a reminder of the importance of humanitarian aid and governments' responsibility to protect their citizens' basic needs during the conflict.

The challenges of post-war — In addition to the lessons above, the Biafra War also provides insights into post-conflict reconciliation and reconstruction challenges. The end of the conflict did not necessarily mean the end of the tensions and grievances that led to the war; rebuilding and healing war wounds was slow and challenging.

The importance of international cooperation in preventing and resolving conflicts-. International efforts to provide humanitarian aid and support mediation efforts were instrumental in preventing the conflict from spreading beyond Nigeria's borders and helping to resolve the war.

The world can learn from the difficulties encountered during post-conflict reconstruction in Nigeria and other countries. These challenges include addressing the root causes of conflict, promoting justice and reconciliation, and building inclusive and transparent institutions. Additionally, it is important to provide participating marginalised groups and communities opportunities to prevent future conflicts.

Like all wars, the Biafra War was a tragic and avoidable conflict that resulted in a significant loss of life and suffering. However, it also offers important lessons for the world to learn, including the dangers of ethnic and religious divisions, the importance of democracy and peaceful resolution of conflicts, and the responsibility of governments to protect the basic needs of their citizens. By learning from past mistakes, we can work towards a more peaceful and equitable future for all.

6.3. LESSONS FROM NIGERIA ABOUT MANAGING PANDEMICS

As of the end of 2021, Nigeria accounted for only 3,155 deaths reported globally despite containing 200 million people. Nigeria's comparatively low mortality rate from COVID-19 significantly defies early predictions of a mass COVID-19 catastrophe and shows that Nigeria has salient lessons to teach the rest of the world.

At the beginning of the COVID-19 pandemic, there were many predictions of doom and gloom for Nigeria. Experts feared that the country's weak healthcare systems, high poverty rates, and lack of clean water and sanitation would be particularly vulnerable to the virus. These predictions led to concerns that Nigeria could face a devastating outbreak, with thousands of deaths on the street and widespread economic devastation.

However, as the pandemic progressed, it became clear that these dire predictions did not come to fruition. Despite initial fears, the number of confirmed COVID-19 cases and deaths in Nigeria has been relatively low compared to other regions.

This book believes that analysing factors that helped Nigeria to experience low morbidity and mortality from COVID-19 are essential and valuable global public health lessons.

Early Government Measures and Messaging: Nigerian governments enacted early response measures to the pandemic: on 5 February 2020, even before a single case was reported in the country. On 22 April 2020, the World Health Organization (WHO) highlighted examples of how African countries were leading the global response. By 15 April 2020, Nigeria had at least five 'stringent public health and social measures' to prepare for the emerging pandemic. Early border closures and lockdowns were enforced, resulting in less international connectivity to prevent viral importation from international flight arrivals. All these had an important early impact on slowing the spread.

Nigerian governments were able to implement this quickly because destructive epidemics are not a new phenomenon in Nigeria. The country constantly deals with abundant infectious diseases (e.g., malaria, yellow fever, tuberculosis, Ebola, and polio). Due to their familiarity with these epidemics. The government has developed effective public health programs with messaging to unify the community and highlight the need for preventative action among individuals. Unlike the governmental mistrust in the western world, Nigerian's population is better prepared to adhere to government public health recommendations.

Population Distribution and Structure of Social Networks: It is well documented that the COVID-19 burden is heavily skewed towards older populations. Nigeria is fortunate because the country has the youngest population, with a median age of 20. In addition, culturally, few older Nigerian people live in nursing homes, unlike the US or the UK, where one-third to one-half of deaths occur in elderly nursing homes.

More than half of Nigeria still lives in rural areas, usually well-spaced houses, well-ventilated and with natural vegetation. Since infected persons usually transmit the virus through coughing, sneezing, talking, singing, and breathing, studies show that coronavirus transmission is concentrated in indoor settings, up to 19 times more than outdoors. As a result, built environments in rural areas well-ventilated with outside air significantly reduce the chance of viral transmission compared to tightly enclosed indoor spaces in developed countries, especially during the cold winter. In contrast, most of Nigeria's deaths happen to the social and political elites that live and work in airconditioned closed spaces in the cities. In addition, people that live in the rural area primarily tend to be farmers, and this profession favours dawn-to-dusk outdoor lifestyles. Prolonged, year-round outdoor living with direct exposure to sun and UV light in Nigeria also reduced transmission, with the additional benefit of vitamin D produced by the sun.

Trained Immunity: The phenomenon of trained immunity may have reduced the COVID-19 statistics in Nigeria. For example, live vaccines activate innate immune systems, protecting against future infections from other pathogens. Recent data suggest countries like Nigeria, where BCG vaccinations are mandatory, have lower COVID-19 disease burden.

The "Hygiene Hypothesis" is the hypothesis that Nigeria's general poor hygiene may have helped reduce COVID-19 infection. Studies show that some environments provide their populations advantages against certain forms of infection and disease due to chronic exposure to a multi-microbial and dirty environment. Over time, this compels their body to produce protective immune effects when encountering new pathogens.

While cleanliness is often preferred and next to Godliness, there has been some concern regarding countries that are overly clean and regularly use ultra-hygienic practices, exemplified by the overuse of hand sanitiser and other disinfection practices. Nigeria is regarded as one of the most vulnerable countries to infectious disease epidemics. As a result, Nigeria's population carries the heaviest burden of infectious diseases. For example, infection by malaria alone may have helped to strengthen the human immune system of Nigeria further and make their body defiant to new diseases, thereby conferring an immune advantage to the populace. This becomes an advantage compared to a population overly prevented from such exposure. That was why President Trump, at the beginning of COVID-19, suggested anti-malaria tablets to cure COVID-19.

Nigeria's use of traditional medicine during COVID — Traditional medicine comprises of unscientific knowledge systems that developed over generations within various societies before the era of Western medicine. Many traditional medicine practitioners in Africa have gained knowledge of medicinal plants and their effects on the human body. Such knowledge is passed on orally from father to son through generations. The components of traditional medicine encompass herbal medicine, therapeutic fasting and dieting, and more. The practitioners include herbalists, diviners and midwives.

Natural Medicine for Primary Care and its effectiveness in Nigeria during the pandemic triggered a World Health Organisation (WHO-AFRO) expert panel in September 2020 to endorse a protocol for the clinical investigation of herbal medicine for COVID-19.

Modern pharmaceuticals and medical procedures have remained unaffordable and inaccessible to many Nigerians due to their relatively high cost. Traditional medicine has become the natural alternative for many Nigerians, as it is affordable and accessible to ordinary Nigerians in rural and urban areas. The remedies made from indigenous plants play a crucial role in the health of millions of Africans. One estimate puts the number of Africans routinely using traditional medicine services as their first choice before Western medicine to be as high as 85% in Sub-Saharan Africa.

Nigeria has joined China, India, the US, and the WHO to undertake in-depth research into traditional herbal medicines' efficacy, safety, quality, standardisation and regulation so that all can accept it.

Genetics: Some genetic and immunological factors could have played a role in shielding Nigeria from the brunt of the pandemic. Studies have shown that African populations have an exceptionally high proportion of O-positivity, at nearly 50%, higher than White and Asian populations. It is possible that this increased O prevalence has conferred a greater protective effect in Nigerian populations compared with other groups with less O prevalence.

In conclusion, the relatively low severity and death due to COVID-19 in Nigeria, the most populous country in Africa, presents somewhat of a paradox. While the media says very little about it, it is a great success that Nigeria and other African countries should be proud of and talk about, as there are many lessons to be learnt by the rest of the world from Nigeria and Africa.

6.4. NIGERIA AND BIRD FLU

Nigeria was the first African country affected by the H5N1 virus (bird flu) outbreaks in 2008. In 2008, the disease rapidly spread to 97 local government areas in Nigeria. The bird flu outbreak caused millions of birds to be lost through deaths and bird culling. In response, the international institutions advised all African chicken-producing countries to cull and kill all their birds to stop the spread to humans. While other African countries yielded this advice, the Nigerian government realised that if they killed all the birds, it would destroy her poultry industries. Nigeria would be left dependent on importing frozen chickens. So, Nigeria refused, while all other West African countries around Nigeria, of course, did. And right now, all these countries, Ghana, Togo, Benin and Cameroon, are importers of frozen chicken while Nigeria is not.

7. Current Economic State of Affairs

Nigeria is the largest economy in Africa and the 30th in the world, with a GDP of more than $400 billion. It is also Africa's most populous state, with a population of 200 million. Nigeria ranks 49th in the export market globally, with exports of $47.6B and imports of $34.2B. Despite ranking top in Africa, Nigeria is the 124th most complex economy, as it remains fragile and susceptible to imported inflation due to the over-dependence on oil exports.

The Nigerian economy is broadly classified into formal and informal sectors. Business analysts estimate that the informal sector accounts for 60% of the economy. However, the informal sector is not included in GDP calculations because it consists primarily of cash-based activities and lacks credible data. This means that when the South African economy is compared with Nigeria, it is only compared with 35% of its formal economy. Nigeria's formal sector economic activities are conducted across several sectors, including agriculture agriculture, services, and manufacturing.

Nigeria is a country of great potential, but it is also a country facing a range of challenges. This chapter will examine the current economic state of affairs in Nigeria, including the country's economy, politics, and security situation and how these issues impact ordinary Nigerians' lives.

The Federal Republic of Nigeria shipped $47.6 billion worth of goods around the globe in 2021. This dollar amount reflects a 16% increase since 2017, but the naira depreciated by 32%. Weaker local currency makes the cost of export more expensive in Nigeria. Nigeria's biggest export is crude oil, representing over three-quarters (76.2%) of its total exported goods by value.

The latest available country-specific data shows that the following countries bought products exported from Nigeria: India (15.9%), Spain (10.7%), France (7.9%), Netherlands (10.1%), Canada (4.5%), United States of America (6.1%), Italy (4%), Indonesia (3.9%), and mainland China (3.9%).

Nigeria major export destinations (2018)

© Encyclopædia Britannica, Inc.

From a continental perspective, 39.8% of Nigeria's exports by value were delivered to European countries, while 34% were sold to importers in Asia. Nigeria shipped another 12.9% worth of goods within Africa. Smaller percentages went to North America (8.8%) and Latin America (4.3%), excluding Mexico.

Given Nigeria's population of 200 million people, the total $47.6 billion in 2021 Nigerian exports translates to roughly $215 for every person, and that dollar metric exceeds the average $160 per capita for 2020. Nigeria is an increasingly important market and manufacturing centre for the African consumer product sector, and Nigeria is home to a growing middle class of about 50 million people.

7.1. NIGERIA'S TOP 10 EXPORTS

The following export product groups represent the highest dollar value in Nigerian global shipments during 2021 and the percentage share each export category represents in terms of overall exports from Nigeria.

Mineral fuels, including oil — $47.6 billion (76.2% of total exports). Nigeria has some of the largest natural gas deposits in the world, with 180 trillion cubic feet of proven reserves. However, the country is yet to mobilize that gas for the domestic market. Political interference, delays in legislating key issues, and an inconsistent approach to regulating the price of gas collectively deterred the necessary investments from capturing and delivering gas to domestic markets. Nigeria has 18 operating pipelines and an average daily production of 1.8 million barrels in 2021.

Ships, boats: $1.4 billion (13%) Nigeria currently has about ten shipyards, with a combined capacity of 66,050T. They include Starz Marine and Engineering Limited, Nigerdock, West Atlantic Shipyard, Naval Dockyard, West African drydocks, Shipside.

Zinc: $258.8 million (0.5%) In 2020, Nigeria exported $31.7M in zinc ore, making it the world's 32nd largest exporter of zinc ore. The main destinations of zinc ore exports from Nigeria are China ($31M), Belgium ($718k), and South Africa ($329k).

Fertilizers: $949.8 million (2%) Since the inauguration of the Dangote Fertiliser Plant in Lagos, Nigeria has commenced the exportation of urea-based fertiliser to the U.S., India, Brazil, Mexico and Argentina.

Oil seeds: $326.2 million (0.7%) Nigeria's export of oil seeds and oleaginous fruits; miscellaneous grains, seeds and fruit; industrial or medicinal usage

Aluminium: $190.3 million (0.4%), making it the world's 38th largest exporter of aluminium ore. The main destinations of aluminium ore exports from Nigeria are: Ghana and Niger

Aircraft, spacecraft: $143.7 million (0.3%) Primarily the re-export of aviation-related equipment (e.g. planes, plane parts, helicopter and helicopter parts) to other countries.

Tobacco manufactured substitutes: $112.8 million (0.2%) The British American Tobacco (BAT) Nigeria's yearly export of tobacco from its facilities to about 14 African countries.

Lead: $94.1 million (0.2%) An estimated 10 million tonnes of lead are spread over Abia, Abuja, Akwa Ibom, Anambra, Bayelsa, Benue, Cross River, Ebonyi, Enugu, Kano, Niger, Plateau and Taraba.

Ores, slag, ash: $63.3 million (Up by 721.3%) About 3 billion metric tonnes of iron ore in the country, the largest deposit, is found in Kogi state. The National Iron Ore Mining companies are Ajaokuta Steel and Delta Steel Company in Aladja.

Copper: $42.7 million (Reversing a -$33.9 million deficit)

Raw hides, leather skins, not fur skins: $23 million (Reversing a -$55.9 million deficit)

7.2. NIGERIA'S MINERAL DISTRIBUTION

Nigeria is endowed with at least 34 solid minerals (about 14 metallic minerals) identified in about 450 locations around the country. Every state in the federation has a fair share of solid mineral deposits; major solid mineral resources in Nigeria are shown below. However, most of the mineral reserves are undeveloped or, at best under-developed.

Figure 1: An overview of the solid mineral resources' distribution map of Nigeria (Adapted from Obaje, 2009; p. 118)

The government has identified seven strategic minerals for exploration. They include bitumen, gold, coal, iron ore, limestone, lead/zinc ores, limestone and barytes. Other minerals with good economic prospects for mining are tin, tantalite, niobite (columbite), gypsum, gemstones, kaolin, etc. These minerals are mined, processed and marketed at less than 5% utilization of the available resources, which means the minerals are untapped despite high local and international demand.

Unfortunately, most mining and processing of minerals is entirely in private expatriates' hands. At the same time, indigenous companies and entrepreneurs contribute little to the nation's revenue, and this does not encourage the growth of local capacity and competence. Again, raw minerals are still being exported out of the country without value addition, and this scenario increases unemployment and attracts meagre foreign exchange to the nation. Building and encouraging local capacities to reverse this trend is necessary.

7.3. PRODUCTS CAUSING WORST TRADE DEFICITS FOR NIGERIA

Nigeria incurred an overall -$4.9 billion deficit for 2021. Below are goods exported to Nigeria that results in negative net exports or product trade balance deficits. These negative net exports reveal product categories where foreign spending on Nigerian country's goods trail Nigerian importer spending on foreign products.

1. Machinery, including computers: -US$7.4 billion
2. Vehicles: -$3.4 billion
3. Electrical machinery, equipment: -$3.1 billion
4. Cereals: -$2.8 billion
5. Plastics, plastic articles: -$2.5 billion
6. Pharmaceuticals: -$1.4 billion
7. Articles of iron or steel: -$1.2 billion
8. Optical, technical, and medical apparatus: -$1.11 billion
9. Sugar, sugar confectionery: -$986.1 million
10. Other chemical goods: -$930.8 million

Nigerian Export Companies

Five Nigerian corporations rank among Forbes Global 2000, including three regional banks, an insurance conglomerate and a construction materials firm.

- Dangote Cement (construction materials)

- Equity Assurance (financial institution)

- FBN Holdings (regional bank)

- Guaranty Trust Bank (regional bank)

- Zenith Bank (regional bank)

Source: Nairametrics

7.4. TOP AGRICULTURAL EXPORTS IN NIGERIA

Nigeria's agricultural sector employs nearly 70% of the population and comprises nearly 22% of the GDP. Nigeria has abundant arable land and a favourable climate for producing nuts, fruits, tubers, and grains. Most farming in Nigeria is subsistence-based, utilizing manual labour and relatively little agricultural machinery. Nigeria continues maintaining import restrictions (high duties, levies, quotas, and import bans) on several agricultural products, including poultry, beef, pork, and rice.

Here is the breakdown of Nigeria's top agricultural exports and top destination countries.

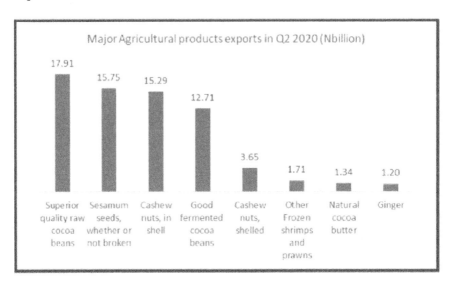

Cocoa: In 2020, Nigeria exported $489M in Cocoa (Fermented, superior quality raw cocoa beans), making it the 5th largest exporter of cocoa beans worldwide. The leading destination of cocoa bean exports from Nigeria are the Netherlands ($157M), Germany ($91.3M), Malaysia ($60.1M), Indonesia ($46M), and Russia ($26.6M).

Sesamum seeds: the tiny, oil-rich seeds, Nigeria made the sum of N112.8 billion from exporting these products. Top destinations for the product include Japan, China, Turkey, India, and Vietnam.

Cashew nuts (In shell and shelled): In 2020, Nigeria generated a total sum of N38.2 billion from cashew nuts export. The top destinations are Vietnam, India, the USA, Russia and the Netherlands.

Frozen shrimps and prawns: Nigeria exported N9.85 billion to the Netherlands, Belgium, France, Vietnam, and the USA.

Natural cocoa butter: Nigeria generated N7.69 billion as revenue proceeds from the export of cocoa butter. Germany and Estonia are top destinations for the product

Sesame oil and its fractions: Sesame oil is an edible vegetable oil derived from sesame seeds with an estimated export value of N3.1 billion

Other agricultural products include

Cotton export, **Agro-food items** (N1.97 billion),

Cut flowers and flower buds (1.96 billion)

Ginger (N1.43 billion).

Source: Nairametrics

7.5. CROPS PRODUCED IN NIGERIA

Nigeria is rich in agricultural resources, with a climate and soil supporting the growth of a wide range of crops. Below are the most important crops produced in Nigeria:

Groundnut Production — the leading producing states include: Niger, Kano, Jigawa, Zamfara, Kebbi, Sokoto, Katsina, Kaduna, Adamawa, Yobe, Borno, Taraba, Plateau, Nasarawa, Bauchi, and Gombe States (NAERL, 2011)

Oil Palm in Nigeria — the main oil palm producing states are: Cross River, Akwa Ibom, Ekiti, Delta, Bayelsa, Ogun, Rivers, Anambra, Ondo, Enugu, Imo, Oyo, Abia, Edo, Ogun, with Cross River, Delta, Ondo and Edo being the highest exporters in commercial quantity

Cocoa-leading producing states are Ekiti, Ogun, Ondo, Osun and Edo, Cross River,

Wheat — Nigeria's northern states of Bornu, Yobe, Jigawa, Kano, Zamfara, Katsina, Adamawa, Sokoto and Kebbi are major wheat-growing areas. Nigeria's domestic wheat production is small, at 70,000 tons.

Cattle Hide and Beef — Nigeria's cattle and cattle-related products are sourced from the Northern portions of the country, in states like Adamawa, Bauchi, Gombe, Niger, Kaduna, Zamfara, Borno, Taraba, Jigawa, Kebbi and Nassarawa. Nigeria has Africa's 4th largest cattle population, estimated at 20 million.

Poultry — According to the CBN, the poultry industry is the country's biggest agricultural sub-sector, with a market size of about $4 billion. The chicken population is estimated to be 165 million birds, producing approximately 650,000 and 300,000 metric tons of eggs and meat, respectively. Nonetheless, this falls short of the demand for over 200 million birds, 790,000 tons of eggs, and 1,500,000 tons of meat. Despite the government ban on imported poultry, smugglers have continued to exploit the supply gap to bring in products through Nigeria's porous land borders. Opportunities exist for poultry production and feed milling machinery, incubators, extruders, feed additives, livestock health drugs and vaccines, and chicken processing equipment.

Pig, Pork – Nigeria is the largest producer of pork meat in Africa, and it has remained underutilised . The ecology of the country's northern and southern parts makes it suitable for pig keeping, but Muslims are forbidden to eat pork.

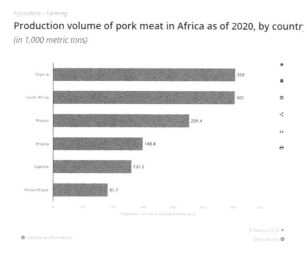

Agriculture > Farming

Production volume of pork meat in Africa as of 2020, by country
(in 1,000 metric tons)

Country	Production volume in thousand metric tons
Nigeria	303
South Africa	302
Malawi	226.4
Angola	149.8
Uganda	131.2
Mozambique	91.7

© Statista 2023

Sorghum — Nigeria is the largest sorghum producer in Africa, accounting for about 71% of the total regional sorghum output, 30-40% of total African production, and is the second largest world producer after the United States. Zamfara, Niger, Plateau, Katsina, Kaduna, Benue, Kano, Bauchi, and Borno are the main producing states. In 2021, Sorghum farmers realized gross margins of over $169 million

Tomato — Nigeria ranked 16th on the global tomato production scale, accounting for 10.79% of Africa's and 1.2% of the total world production of tomatoes. While tomatoes are cultivated in most states, Jigawa, Katsina, Zamfara, Sokoto, Kaduna, Bauchi, Gombe, Taraba, and Kano are leading the pack in the commercial cultivation of the crop. In 2021, farmers increased tomato production by 26% to national production. In 2021, tomato farmers realized gross margins of over $53 million.

Timber and Wood Products Production — Nigeria's major wood processing industries are typically large capacity facilities such as large sawmills, plywood mills, pulp and paper plants and large numbers of small-scale wood product manufacturing companies such as furniture industries, cabinet makers and carpentry. Round wood in Nigeria comes mostly from the natural high forest zone of the country, in particular from the Southern States of Nigeria, but most especially in Ondo, Cross River, Ogun, Edo, Delta Ekiti, Osun and Oyo States of Nigeria, which are the largest producers. The most important wood products produced, consumed and traded in Nigeria are sawn-wood, plywood, particle board, newsprint, printing and writing paper and other paper boards

Pepper — The greater part of pepper production in Nigeria is undertaken in the northern areas, in Kaduna, Kano, Jigawa, Katsina, Sokoto, Plateau and Bauchi states. The natural features of these regions, especially the presence of flood-prone plains and river basins and, above all, the development of vast irrigated lands, create conditions that greatly favour the development of this crop

Rubber — The Bulk of Nigeria's Rubber production come from the Southern states of Delta, Edo, Ondo, Ogun, Cross River

Soybean — Soybean was first introduced to Ibadan, Oyo State, Nigeria, in 1908. Nigeria is the largest crop producer of human, and livestock feeds in West and Central Africa. The country's major soybean-producing states are Benue, Kaduna, Taraba, Plateau and Niger in the central regions. Other growing areas include Nasarawa, Kebbi, Kwara, Oyo, Jigawa, Borno, Bauchi, Lagos, Sokoto, Zamfara and FCT. The yield of soybean is 1,700 kg per hectare on research plots in Nigeria

Maize/Corn — Maize/Corn is grown widely throughout the country. The Central states of Nigeria such as Niger, Kaduna, Taraba, Plateau, Adamawa

Cowpea is grown in Nigeria at varying degrees, but the crop seems to do best in the drier climates of the northern regions. Nigeria is Africa's largest cowpea/pulses producer and the 4th largest producer in the world after India, Canada and Burma. The major growing/production areas in Nigeria are: Borno, Zamfara, Sokoto, Kano, Gombe and Yobe

Cashew/ Cashew nut production — Since 2008, Nigeria has become the largest producer of cashew nuts in the world. Nigeria was last the largest producer of cashew in 2010. Cashew nut production trends have varied over the decades. At the same time, Nigeria is the world's 6th largest producer of cashew fruits, with an annual production volume of about 120,000 tonnes. The Cashew Industry also provides about 600,000 jobs and a total annual trade worth N24 billion, thus making the sector a major contributor to Nigeria's non-oil GDP. It is widely grown in the southern states of Nigeria. Especially: Enugu, Oyo, Anambra, Kogi, Osun, Abia, Ondo, Benue, Cross River, Imo, Ekiti, Ebonyi, Kwara

Cassava production — Cassava (Manihot esculenta) production is vital to the economy of Nigeria as the country is the world's largest producer of the commodity. The crop is produced in 24 of the country's 36 states. In 1999, Nigeria produced 33 million tonnes, while a decade later, it produced approximately 45 million tonnes, almost 19% of the production in the world. The average yield per hectare is 10.6 tonnes. And it is a staple in many parts of the country. In Nigeria, cassava production is well-developed as an organized agricultural crop. It has well-established multiplication and processing techniques for food products and cattle feed. Imo, Ondo, Anambra, Kogi, Taraba, Cross River, Enugu, Ogun, Benue, Delta, and Edo are the main producing states. In 2021, Cassava farmers realized more than $55 million as revenue and a gross margin of over $36 million

Yam Production — Nigeria is by far the world's largest producer of yams, accounting for over 70–76% of the world's production. According to the Food and Agricultural Organization report, in 1985, Nigeria produced 18.3 million tonnes of yam from 1.5 million hectares, representing 73.8% of total yam production in Africa. According to 2008 figures, yam production in Nigeria has nearly doubled since 1985, with Nigeria producing 35.017 million metric tonnes with a value equivalent of US$5.654 billion. The major yam-producing states in Nigeria are Adamawa, Benue, Cross River, Delta, Edo, Ekiti, Imo, Kaduna, Kwara, Ogun, Ondo, Osun, Oyo, and Plateau. Benue state is, however, the largest producer.

Cotton — As a major cash crop, cotton is of considerable social and economic importance to Nigeria. Cotton/textile activities are widespread in the country. Cotton production in Nigeria dates back to 1903, with the British Cotton Growers Association taking the lead until 1974. The traditional cotton growing areas are concentrated in Northern and South Western Nigeria. In the Savannah belts of the country: Kaduna, Ondo, Kano, Katsina, Oyo, Kwara, Ogun Zamfara, Jigawa, Sokoto, Kebbi

Seafood Production — Mainly shrimps, periwinkles, clams, oysters, crayfish etc. The main producer states are Lagos, Ogun, Ondo, Edo, Bayelsa, Rivers Akwa Ibom and Cross River located in the coastal zone.

Rice Production — Nigeria is West Africa's largest rice producer. The rice-producing areas can be subdivided into the rainfed upland (30%), The rainfed lowlands AKA "Fadama (47%), irrigated (17%), and deep water floating production (5%). The main areas of rice cultivation in the country include the middle belt and Northern states of Benue, Borno, Kaduna, Kano, Niger and Taraba, as well as the South Eastern states of Enugu, Cross River and Ebonyi. Kaduna is the main producing state, followed by Niger, Benue, Ebonyi, Taraba, Kano and Borno. The latter seven states account for over 67% of total rice production in the country. In 2021, farmers increased rice production by 27% and realized gross margins of over $288 million

Citrus Production — In Nigeria, about 3.4 million metric tonnes of citrus fruits are produced annually (2013) from an estimated 3 million hectares of land (FAO, 2008). The country is the 9th major citrus fruit-producing country globally after Italy. Major citrus-producing states in Nigeria include Benue, Nassarawa, Kogi, Ogun, Oyo, Osun, Ebonyi, Kaduna, Taraba, Ekiti, Imo, Kwara, Edo, and Delta in that order. Oranges account for most citrus production, but significant quantities of grapefruits, lemons and limes are also grown. , The fruit industry in Nigeria began under the western regional government of Chief Obafemi Awolowo in the 1950s. As a result of the downturn in the cocoa trade and subsequent pervasive microbiological attacks, the government decided to start a pilot project in cultivating citrus and other fruits primarily to provide farmers with an alternative source of income. Thus, the Lafia canning factory in Ibadan was born in 1954, and to feed the factory, Apoje Citrus Farm was established, backed by an aggressive farm settlement scheme. Interestingly, this has been bought by Funman Agricultural Product Ltd, and it serves as its manufacturing base. From that small beginning in the 1950s, fruit juice manufacturing in Nigeria has taken a giant leap.

Sugar and Sugarcane Production Sugar cane production is mainly located in the border states of Kano, Kaduna and Kastina, representing respectively 8%, 13% and 13% of the domestic production. Two other regions remain important in terms of production: (Kebbi and Sokoto) as well as the North East (Taraba and Adamawa).

Banana and Plantain Production, Nigeria is one of Africa's largest banana and plantain (Mussa .spp) growing countries. Nigeria produces 2.74 million tonnes of bananas annually, according to the Food and Agriculture Organisation (FAO). It is also the largest plantain-producing country in West Africa, making the crop one of the important staples in the country. The main banana and plantain growing regions in Nigeria are found in the South and Central regions of Nigeria, the largest quantities are produced in Edo, Ondo, Delta, and Ogun States. Other producing states are Rivers, Cross River, Oyo, Akwa Ibom, Ebonyi, Ekiti, Imo, Plateau, Osun, Bayelsa, Kogi, Abia, Anambra and Enugu. Plantain cultivation is not limited to big plantation but is often grown in small orchards, which sometimes go unnoticed

7.6. **FOOD IMPORTATION IN NIGERIA**

Nigeria relies on $10 billion of imports to meet its food and agricultural production shortfalls (primarily wheat, rice, poultry, fish, food services, and consumer-oriented foods). Europe, Asia, the United States, South America, and South Africa are major sources of agricultural imports.

Nigeria's agricultural sector has been hurt by several shocks: sporadic flooding, Boko Haram (BH) insurgencies, banditry, kidnapping, insurgency in Nigeria's agriculture belt and conflicts between herdsmen and local farmers. This has led to food price inflation rising to 22.95% in 2021 on staple food such as cereals, yams, meat, fish, and fruits. Also, higher fuel prices have contributed to rising food prices. In addition, food processing continues to suffer from a lack of financing and infrastructure.

Wheat — Nigeria is the fifth largest U.S. wheat importer in the world. Bread, semolina, and pasta are staples in Nigeria, and the demand for these products continues to increase. Local wheat production meets an insignificant portion of Nigeria's wheat consumption demand. Nigeria has seen prices of all locally grown staple foods spike in 2021, weakening consumer purchasing power and forcing consumers to resort to cheaper commodities.

Rice — Nigeria is Africa's largest rice producer and among the top 15 producers. However, the high cost of rough paddy rice and high operational costs continue to hamper large-scale, integrated rice mills from producing at competitive prices. Imports continue to meet approximately half of the country's rice demand. Thailand- and India-origin rice (long-grain varieties) dominate imports. Nigeria remains one of the world's largest markets for parboiled rice — consuming on average of $4.0 billion worth of parboiled rice each year.

Dairy — The size of Nigeria's dairy market in 2019 was $1.6 billion, with over 87% of demand met through imports. Nigeria has Africa's 4th largest cattle population, estimated at 20 million cattle, including 2.35 million cows used for dairy production. The reconstituted milk is mostly packaged and sold as powdered, evaporated, and condensed milk and packaged in metal cans and sachets of different weights.

Frozen Seafood — Frozen seafood is Nigerians' most affordable source of animal protein, and consumption is increasing. The country is a potential market for approximately 2.5 million metric tons of fish valued at $3 billion. The main species consumed are Atlantic mackerel, horse mackerel, herring, and croakers. Domestic catches and aquaculture production (mainly catfish and tilapia) remain underdeveloped due to high input costs

Nigeria is progressing in its agriculture; according to the World Bank, over 7 million farmers received improved agricultural technology. A Farmers' Microfinance Bank birthed from

FADAMA gives loans at a low-interest rate of 3.5% for business startup and expansion, with an 80% recovery rate. The amount saved from the FADAMA enterprises was over $200,000 as of 2019. 3,102 hectares received improved irrigation services through the ongoing rehabilitation of 3 dams located in Sokoto, Zamfara, and Kano states under the Transforming Irrigation Management in Nigeria project

7.7. CAN NIGERIA BE THE BREADBASKET OF AFRICA

According to FAO, Nigeria has 70.8 million hectares of agricultural land. At present, only half of the 34 million hectares of arable land are cultivated, and another 6.5 million hectares are for permanent crops, leaving 30 million acres of land yet to be cultivated.

The size of land yet to be cultivated in Nigeria is nearly as big as Ukraine's total agricultural land, which has around 42 million hectares (and is also called "the breadbasket of Europe"), and it is as big as Italy's total agricultural land, which is 33 million hectares.

Given the size and fertility of Nigeria's farmland and the vast scope for increased harvests and greater efficiency through ongoing modernization, it is no exaggeration to state that Nigeria can feed Africa. As mentioned earlier, Nigeria is currently a leader in various types of agricultural production and is also a large global exporter in this sector.

However, Nigeria faces many challenges that affect its agricultural productivity and food security, such as poor land tenure system, low level of irrigation farming, climate change and land degradation.

Adding Value to Agriculture

Local agricultural processing is vital to the country's food production. While Nigerian farmers put a lot of effort into their crops or livestock, they tend to get the least out of it when it comes to the market. For a long time, local farmers have been comfortable with the way they have been handling agricultural produce. Most foods have been eaten fresh, and any leftovers are thrown away; there hasn't been any urgency before to consume food efficiently, let alone preserve it. There is a belief that this trend can be reversed only through value addition, from input to production to processing, marketing, logistics financing etc.

According to Mr Adesina, "*agriculture is no longer a way of life for Africans. It is a business, a wealth-creating sector. Africa spends $35 billion annually importing food it could produce by itself, and it is estimated that Africa will spend another $110 billion importing food within the next five years.*"

He continued, "*Africa has to add value to everything it produces and create wealth for herself. Africa accounts for 75% of the global production of cocoa. Still, Africa gets only 2% of a $100 billion chocolate market. While the price of cocoa is falling and cocoa farmers in Africa are losing billions of dollars, the price of chocolate remains the same and never goes down. Also, the price of cotton keeps falling while the cost of textiles is never going down. Coffee beans also drop, but never the price of brewed coffee. Africa has to develop its agricultural value chains to add value to everything it produces. This would lead to a sustainable, solid rural sector*".

Value-added Agriculture is a worthwhile investment that can generate higher returns, allow penetration of a new potentially high-value market, extend the production season, create a brand identity and develop brand loyalty. Value-added agriculture generally focuses on production or manufacturing processes, marketing or services that increase the value of primary agricultural produce, perhaps by increasing appeal to the consumer and the consumer's willingness to pay a premium over similar but undifferentiated products.

However, processing capacity alone does no good without sufficient local production volumes of raw materials. Processing capacity must grow alongside local production, essential for achieving food security and more efficient markets in Nigeria.

There are many constraints to value addition, even where economic arguments are strong. First is a lack of resources, including refrigeration, cold storage, vehicles, and skilled personnel. Then there are deficient or confusing standards, especially between countries. And there are serious health dangers to some locally-grown produce, such as aflatoxin that can be found in large quantities in maise and nuts.

In summary, there are many challenges to adding value to agricultural products in Nigeria, but so are the benefits that value addition will bring to Nigerian farmers. They include;

- Increased revenue. Any addition adds a percentage of increased financial value to the product and improves the incomes of the local farmers.

- Value addition allows the farmer to focus on the consumer while producing; by meeting expectations, he can create a loyal market around the product.

- The marketing bill is the difference between farm gate value and retail value, and it is growing bigger by the day. It consists of processing, marketing, and transportation, and it is a good idea if the producer could get a share, especially on the processing side.

- Increased shelf life is a benefit any farmer would want. The longer the product can stay without getting spoiled, the more the guarantee one has of a product selling at their preferred price and time. Milk, for instance, hardly lasts over 24 hours, but with boiling, it can last more days, while with further processing into ghee, the same milk can last months.

- With value addition comes increased bargaining power.

- Brand creation is one of the de facto results of value addition. Your product can be directly identified with you or your farm, which is important in an industry where customers exercise a lot of brand loyalty. It allows customers to always and readily identify with you and win you more referral customers.

To ensure that farmers reap maximum benefits from value addition, the government would need to do the following;

- Train farmers on better post-harvest handling of produce since that is the start of the journey towards a good product on the market.

- Train farmers on multiple processing alternatives.

- Create village farmers (clusters) teams that can collectively combine their expertise and resources to engage in a value addition exercise.

- Harnesses indigenous food processing technologies already embedded in the local skillsets.

- Educate the farmers on the potential uses of the 'waste' material from processed raw material; for instance, dried banana peels can be used to make animal feeds.

Finally, technology is a key driver of competitiveness, where Nigerian lag far behind their South Asian counterparts. These four pillars of institutions, infrastructure, human capital, and technology will drive Nigeria's manufacturing-led growth.

Post harvest losses

Post-harvest loss refers to the reduction in quantity or quality of agricultural products after they are harvested and before they reach the final consumers. Post-harvest loss can occur at various value chains stages, such as harvesting, handling, processing, storage, transportation and marketing.

According to Ventures Africa, Nigeria and its farmers are losing a fortune to post-harvest loss. The Federal Government recently disclosed that the total cost of post-harvest losses in Nigeria's agriculture industry is N3.5 trillion, equivalent to about 10% of Nigeria's GDP in 2020.

Nigeria annually suffers about 60% post-harvest loss in tomato production and other vegetables. This is due to poor infrastructure, inadequate storage facilities, lack of processing capacity, inefficient market access and low awareness among farmers. According to Blueprint, post-harvest losses pose serious implications for food security in Nigeria, with the country losing about $9 billion annually due to post-harvest losses in the sector. This affects the availability and affordability of food for millions of Nigerians already facing hunger and malnutrition.

To address this challenge, Nigeria must adopt various strategies, such as improving infrastructure and logistics, enhancing storage and processing technologies, promoting value addition and quality standards, strengthening market linkages and information systems, increasing farmer education and extension services, and implementing supportive policies and regulations.

7.8. THE CONTRIBUTION OF MILLENNIALS AND GENERATION Z

In Nigeria, both Millennials and Generation Z represent unique human capital and dynamic generations that will shape the future of Nigeria in significant ways.

Millennials, born between 1981 and 1996, aged between 25 and 35, make up 39% of Nigeria's consumer market and have a lot of power in purchasing decisions. They are often referred to as the "lost generation" due to the significant social, economic, and political changes they have experienced. Despite these challenges, Millennials in Nigeria are highly educated and ambitious; they highly value personal and professional development and are skilled in technology. They are also socially conscious, actively engaged in social and political issues, and critical of the status quo.

Generation Z, was born between 1997 and 2012. Nigeria's age structure indicates over 25% of the 200 million population belongs to Gen Z; they are characterized by their high technological savvy and comfort with digital technologies. They have grown up in a world of instant access to information and pervasive social media use. In Nigeria, Generation Z faces high unemployment and economic insecurity but is also the largest and most educated generation in the country's history. They are entrepreneurial, environmentally conscious, and embrace diversity and inclusivity.

Gen Zs were born during the dot com era and were raised on technology. They witnessed Barrack Obama's election, gender equality, sexual orientation equality, shared family responsibilities, and collective volunteerism. They are often referred to as the "coconut generation". They were born into a deeply troubled system, into a time of worldwide terrorism attacks, Arab uprisings, effects of climate change and a great recession. This generation has come of age to shape policies and open.

Millennials and Generation Z represent two distinct yet overlapping generations in Nigeria, accounting for nearly 60% of the population. With their diverse backgrounds, innovative spirits, and commitment, they are poised to make a positive impact. With their strong work ethic, creativity, and drive to make a positive impact, this generation is poised to play a crucial role in shaping Nigeria's future for the better. They are resilient, optimistic, and committed to positively impacting their communities and the world. Whether through involvement in activism, volunteer work, or the creation of new businesses, these generations are working to create a better future for themselves and those around them.

They both embrace technology and digital communication. They are highly connected, with many using social media and other digital platforms to stay connected with friends, family, and professional networks. They are also comfortable using technology for work and are skilled at using digital tools to be productive and efficient.

Their focus is on personal and professional development. Many young people in this generation are eager to improve their skills and knowledge and actively seek opportunities for growth and advancement. They are also a socially conscious generation highly engaged in social and political issues. They are also environmentally conscious and want to work towards creating a more sustainable future. They are also highly engaged in social and political issues, using social media to raise awareness and mobilize support for causes they believe in.

Data and technology will be the crude oil for Nigeria's millennials and Generation Z. The choice to identify with the growing technology ecosystem has been made simpler by the fluctuations in global oil prices, the corruption inherent in the export and import of petroleum products, irregularities in petrol prices in the country, and the multiplier economy in the e-commerce, payment, and services industry.

These youth are the country's most valuable resource (human capital). Human capital refers to a country's workforce's skills, knowledge, and abilities. Nigeria's human capital has been a topic of discussion in recent years due to the country's rapid population growth, poverty, and high levels of unemployment.

According to the United Nations Development Programme (UNDP), Nigeria ranks 161 out of 189 countries on the Human Development Index (HDI). The HDI measures human well-being and considers life expectancy, education, and income. Nigeria's low HDI score is due to several factors, including inadequate investment in education and health, high levels of poverty, and inequality.

Education is a critical aspect of human capital development. Nigeria has made significant progress in improving access to education over the last decade, with primary school enrolment reaching 72% in 2019, up from 58% in 2008. However, the quality of education remains low, with many students not achieving basic literacy and numeracy skills. There is also a significant gender gap in education, with girls less likely to attend school than boys.

Investment in health is also essential for human capital development. Nigeria has made progress in reducing infant mortality rates, but maternal mortality rates remain high. The country also faces a significant burden of infectious diseases like malaria, tuberculosis, and HIV/AIDS. Healthcare infrastructure, personnel, and technology investment are needed to improve health outcomes and increase human capital.

High levels of poverty and inequality also pose significant challenges to human capital development in Nigeria. Poverty reduces access to education, health, and other essential services and limits opportunities for economic growth and social mobility. Inequality exacerbates these challenges by creating a divide between those with and without access to resources.

How Nigeria can Harness its Human Capital

The future of Nigerian human capital is a critical concern for policymakers, civil society, and the private sector. With a population of over 200 million, Nigeria has one of the largest workforces in the world. However, the country's human capital is currently facing several challenges, including inadequate investment in education and health, high levels of poverty, and inequality.

Nigeria can harness its human capital by investing in education and training and creating youth employment and entrepreneurship opportunities.

Investing in education: Education is key to developing the human capital of Nigeria. By investing in education, the country can provide its citizens with the skills and knowledge they need to compete in the global economy and become active citizens. This can be done through funding for schools, scholarships, and other educational programs.

Skills development: Nigeria must invest in skill development programs to harness its human capital. This can be done through vocational training and apprenticeship programs that provide young people with the practical skills they need to enter the workforce.

Encouraging entrepreneurship: Encouraging entrepreneurship is another way for Nigeria to harness its human capital. Nigeria can create jobs and stimulate economic growth by providing young people with the resources and support they need to start their own businesses.

Promoting employment: Promoting employment is another way to harness human capital in Nigeria. The government can create jobs by investing in infrastructure projects and supporting small and medium-sized enterprises.

Creating incentives for companies to invest in their employees through training and development programs can also help harness human capital in Nigeria, e. g. tax breaks, grants, or other financial incentives.

Attracting foreign investment: Attracting foreign investment is another way to harness human capital in Nigeria. Nigeria can attract foreign companies to provide its citizen's jobs and training opportunities by providing a stable and business-friendly environment.

Leveraging technology: Leveraging technology can help Nigeria to harness its human capital by providing easy access to information, education, and business opportunities. For example, the use of e-learning platforms, online job portals, and virtual marketplaces for entrepreneurs. Another way Nigeria can harness its human capital is by improving the quality of healthcare available to its citizens. A healthy population is productive, and improving access to healthcare can help increase life expectancy and reduce the disease burden. This can be done through increasing funding for healthcare services, building new healthcare facilities, and training more health-care professionals.

Improving its citizens' living standards. This can be done by increasing access to basic services like housing, electricity, and clean water. By providing citizens with better living conditions, they will be more productive and able to contribute more to society.

Promoting gender equality and providing equal opportunities for men and women. This can be done by implementing policies that promote equal pay, increasing the number of women in leadership roles, and providing education and training opportunities for women. By promoting gender equality, Nigeria can tap into the full potential of its human capital, as women constitute a large part of the population.

To address the challenge of poverty and inequality, there is a need for policies that promote inclusive growth and social mobility. These policies should include progressive taxation, social safety nets, and targeted poverty reduction programs. By reducing poverty and inequality, Nigeria can ensure that all its citizens have access to essential services and the opportunity to reach their full potential.

The development of digital skills. As technology continues to transform the global economy, there is a growing demand for workers with digital skills. Nigeria has a young and tech-savvy population, and there is enormous potential to develop a skilled workforce that can drive the country's digital economy.

Finally, the future of Nigerian human capital depends on strong leadership and governance. Nigeria has a rich history of leadership and a legacy of corruption and mismanagement. There is a need for leaders who are committed to the country's long-term development and accountable to their citizens.

In conclusion, the future of Nigerian human capital is a critical concern for the country's long-term development. There is a need for sustained investment in education, health, and poverty reduction, the development of digital skills, and strong leadership and governance. By addressing these challenges, Nigeria can unleash the potential of its human capital and build a brighter future for all its citizens.

8. Nigerian Infrastructure

8.1. SECURITY

Many countries can trace their police and military formations to protect citizens and ensure territorial integrity. However, this is not the case in Africa, especially in Nigeria. The British established the police and military during Colonialism primarily to enforce hateful and debilitating Colonial laws, including to force taxation and crush civilian opposition to Colonial rule.

At the end of Colonialism, the newly independent African government inherited institutions that had internalised a culture of citizen oppression and extortion. Post-independence police and military continued to inflict terror on innocent citizens, and citizens had internalised the art of getting away with any unwarranted harassment or bribing the officer.

Nigeria's present police force is headed by the inspector general of police, appointed by the president. The force's general inefficiency is compounded by the low level of education, the low morale of police recruits, who are also poorly housed and very poorly paid, and the lack of modern equipment. As a result, corruption is widespread.

A more recent example of this terror in Nigeria was witnessed on the 23rd of October 2020, when a group of unarmed youths in Nigeria was protesting the brutality of the Nigerian police unit called SARS, which was accused of torture of young people. The same police, with the military's assistance, came, shot and killed over 53 unarmed youths at Lekki Tollgate in Lagos. It later came to light that the UK government had trained and supplied equipment to Nigeria's 'brutal' police unit accused of torture and extrajudicial killings two years earlier. Here we see an ex-colonial force using British taxpayers' money to undermine human rights and fuel injustice and inequality in Nigeria.

End Sars Police, Nigeria. Source: *www.worldstagenews.com*

Nigeria faces numerous security challenges that have been persistent for many years and have become more complex and multifaceted. These security challenges affect the country's stability, development, and social cohesion. Some of the major security challenges in Nigeria include:

Boko Haram Insurgency: Boko Haram is a jihadist group operating in north-eastern Nigeria since 2009 to establish an Islamic state in Nigeria. The group has carried out numerous attacks on civilians, government officials, and security personnel, causing thousands of deaths and displacing millions of people.

Herder-Farmer Conflicts between herders and farmers over land and resources have escalated in recent years, leading to clashes and violence in various parts of the country. Ethnic and religious differences often fuel these conflicts.

Kidnapping: Kidnapping has become a lucrative business for criminal gangs in Nigeria, who target individuals, especially foreigners, for ransom.

Banditry: Banditry is a term used to describe criminal activities such as armed robbery, theft, and looting carried out by armed groups.

Political Violence: Political violence is a recurring problem in Nigeria, particularly during elections. The use of violence and intimidation by political actors and their supporters to gain power or influence seriously threatens the democratic process and the country's stability.

Cybersecurity: With the rapid growth of technology and the internet in Nigeria, cybersecurity has become a significant concern. Cybercriminals target individuals, businesses, and government agencies stealing personal and financial information and disrupting online activities.

Addressing these security challenges requires a multifaceted approach involving effective law enforcement, community engagement, social and economic development, and regional and international cooperation. The Nigerian government and its partners need to work together to address the root causes of these challenges and provide sustainable solutions to ensure the safety and security of all Nigerians.

8.2. **HEALTH AND WELFARE**

The concentration of people in the cities has created enormous sanitary problems, particularly improper sewage disposal, water shortages, and poor drainage. Large heaps of domestic refuse spill across narrow streets, causing traffic delays; garbage dumping along streambeds constitutes a major health hazard and has contributed to the floods that have often plagued Ibadan, Lagos, and other cities during the rainy season. Diarrheal diseases and malaria are among the leading causes of death, especially among children. Most urban Nigerians source their water via wells or boreholes, which they build along with the house, while rural communities source water from streams or rivers. As a result, they tend to suffer from inadequate or impure water supplies.

The main killers in Nigeria are conditions that are not related to diseases (like malnutrition), nor diseases that the western world considers inconveniences (measles, diarrhoea), nor those which have been virtually eradicated by hygiene or cheap injections (diphtheria, poliomyelitis and tetanus).

There are hospitals in large cities and towns. Most state capitals have specialized hospitals; many are home to a university teaching hospital. The cities have numerous private hospitals, clinics, and maternity centres. There are sometimes medical personnel shortages, modern equipment, and supplies.

Traditional health services in Nigeria are centrally planned and tend to favour big hospitals in the cities rather than "primary health care" (PHC) in rural communities. PHC emphasises education and the hardware of health (piped water, protected wells, sanitation systems, safe food storage) rather than the diseases themselves.

Improving Nigeria's health system

Nigeria can improve its health system by implementing a combination of short-term and long-term solutions:

Good water and sanitation — The western world sometimes perceives Africa as unhealthy and full of many nasty diseases: cholera, malaria, amoebic dysentery, sleeping sickness, snail fever, river blindness, leprosy, and yellow fever. But the reality is that Nigeria's health problems are not caused so much by diseases as by poverty. Wealth determines health, and the poorest are the children. The rate at which infants die indicates both the health and wealth of a nation infant mortality rates correlate closely with national per capita income. Over 80% of all illness in Nigeria is directly or indirectly associated with poor water supply and sanitation. It is estimated that safe drinking water and sanitation could cut infant mortality in half in much of Nigeria. Water scarcity contributes to illness through bad hygiene, which spreads infections that affect the eyes, skin, and gastrointestinal tract. Handwashing can cut diarrhoeal diseases dramatically by 40% in the under-5 age group. Contaminated water carries additional health risks. Those who wash their hands, food, or eating utensils in such water risk catching typhoid, cholera, dysentery, gastro-enteritis, polio and hepatitis.

There is a need for the government to be committed to digging or drilling wells, protecting natural water springs, or building water purification systems, especially in rural areas, to ensure everyone has access to clean water within two miles of wherever they live.

Children drinking water

Increasing Government Funding: One short-term solution to improve Nigeria's health system is to increase government funding for the health sector. About 3% of Nigeria's GDP is currently invested in the health sector, which is considerably less than half of Ghana's average healthcare spending of 7%. Nigeria should allocate a larger portion of the national budget to the health sector to provide resources for hospitals, clinics, and healthcare workers.

A top UN official highlighted that *"if Africa [like] East Asia, adapts to its local context and makes comparable investments in young people, Africa could...[add] as much as 500 billion U.S. dollars to its economy every year for as many as 30 years" resulting in "the total transformation of Africa."*

Increasing Access to Healthcare: Nigeria can increase access to healthcare, particularly for people in rural and underserved areas. Nigeria is the second largest contributor in terms of under-five mortality rates in the world. About 150 children under five die each day in rural areas. Yet three-quarters of governments' health spending is devoted to providing urban dwellers with high-technology care. Concentrating on training too many doctors without complementary health care services is disadvantageous for Nigeria as it puts a big dent in the limited resources. The community health workers will be close enough to encourage people to change their way of life. They can also explain to a villager, whose main concern is day-to-day survival, why she must clean up the house, build a latrine, use precious water for washing, feed the children several times a day, and give them milk or eggs.

A few of the world's least developed countries have managed this kind of low-cost health revolution. India, China, Sri Lanka, and Kerala have all attained "northern" life expectancies without the western level of health investment. In terms of costs and benefits, a number of studies show that African countries can expect the greatest improvement in life expectancies from health investments in maternal and child health services in rural and urban slum areas, costing less than $2 per capita.

Retaining and Improving the Quality of Healthcare Workers: Former South Africa president Thabo Mbeki lamented Africa's brain drain as "frightening." Africa has lost 20,000 academics and 10% of highly skilled professionals every year. The impact of brain drain is particularly pervasive in public service, especially in the health sector. Currently, 40,000 of the 75,000 registered Nigerian doctors and 7,000 Nigerian nurses practice abroad, putting an enormous strain on public health delivery. It was estimated that the economic cost of this migration to each African country is between $21,000 and $59,000 to train a medical doctor. Retaining health workers can be achieved by implementing policies that attract and retain the best healthcare workers, such as providing gainful employment, professional development, and educational opportunities to qualified nationals in their home countries. Also, adherence to

meritocratic recruitment procedures, infrastructure development, better remunerations, and incentive mechanisms to attract and retain highly qualified Nigerians. Ultimately, as President Obama said: *"If we have African leaders, governments, and
institutions that create a platform for success and opportunity,
then Africans will increasingly get more talent wanting to stay...
Once you reach a tipping point, not only will you stop the brain
drain, but it will start reversing"*.

Improving Infrastructure and Equipment: This can be done
by investing in new technologies and equipment, upgrading
existing facilities, providing the demanded power supply,
drinking water, and efficient communication systems and expanding access to essential medicines and vaccines. The government should spend heavy funds on infrastructure and new
hospital equipment.

In conclusion, Nigeria can improve its health system by increasing government funding, improving the quality of healthcare
workers, increasing access to healthcare, improving infrastructure and equipment, encouraging private sector participation,
addressing corruption, and developing a National Health Insurance System. With the right policies and investments, Nigeria can improve its health system and drive its growth and
development in the future.

8.3. HOUSING

Overcrowding in the cities has caused slums to spread and
shantytown suburbs to emerge in mostof the larger urban
centres. Individuals build most houses and because banks do
generally not lend money for home construction, most people
must rely on their savings. A federal housing program provides
funds for the construction of low-cost housing for low- and

middle-income workers in the state capitals, local government headquarters, and other large towns.

Busy Street of Lagos. Source: *www.istockphoto.com*

House types vary by geographic location. In the coastal areas, the walls and roofs are made from the raffia palm, which abounds in the region. Rectangular mud houses with mat roofs are found in the forest belt, although the more prosperous houses have corrugated iron roofs. In the savanna areas of the central region and in parts of the north, houses are round mud buildings roofed with sloping grass thatch, but flat mud roofs appear in the drier areas of the extreme north. Larger houses are designed around an open courtyard and traditionally contain barrels or cisterns where rainwater can be collected.

Regarding housing, Nigeria currently has a housing deficit of 17 million houses. The country is estimated to build at least 700,000 houses annually to close the gap. However, Nigeria currently builds just 2,000 houses per year.

HOUSE IN BANANA ISLAND, IKOYI, LAGOS, NIGERIA.
Source DessyDee Consortium

8.4. EDUCATION

Until 1950, Christian missionary bodies operated most schools, introducing Western-style education into Nigeria in the mid-19th century. The British Colonial government funded a few schools, although its policy was to give mission schools grants rather than expand its own system. In the northern, predominantly Muslim area, Western-style education was prohibited because the religious leaders did not want Christian missionaries interfering with Islam, and Islamic education was provided in traditional Islamic schools.

Today, free and compulsory primary education begins at age six and lasts six years. Secondary education consists of two three-year cycles, the first cycle of which is free and compulsory. Although federal and state governments have the major responsibility for education, other organizations, such as private organisations and religious groups, may establish and administer primary and secondary schools; the state governments control colleges of education and of technology.

At the time of Nigeria's independence in 1960, there were only two established postsecondary institutions, University College at Ibadan (founded in 1948) and Yaba Higher College (founded in 1934.) But now Nigeria has more than 400 universities and colleges widely dispersed throughout the country in an attempt to make higher education easily accessible. Many universities are federally controlled, and the language of instruction is English at all the universities and colleges. In the 1990s, the Federal Ministry of Education approved individuals and private organizations, including various Christian churches, to establish universities, and since then, hundreds of private postsecondary institutions have been established.

Education is the best weapon against impoverishment, disease, early marriage, gang activities, and prostitution. Educated children stand a better chance of having opportunities for constructive and positive life paths. Educated teenage women are less likely to marry early and become very young mothers, and educated people are less likely to fall victim to a preventable disease

However, it is critical to promote an education system that is "fit for purpose" with a strong focus on entrepreneurship and technology to optimise opportunities. The potential for Nigeria to leverage its human capital lies in its ability to invest in the education and training of children and young people. Investments in education will help break intergenerational poverty cycles and aid socio-economic development; it will lead to a qualified and employable workforce that meets the demands of the labour markets for skills and competencies.

Nigeria can learn from the examples of the economy of the four "Asian Tigers." Studies have shown that the economies of South Korea, Hong Kong, Singapore, and Taiwan maintained high growth rates and rapid industrialisation between the early 1960s and 1990s. Education was singled out as a key factor for improving their productivity. These territories focused on improving the education system at all levels; heavy emphasis was placed on ensuring that all children attended compulsory elementary and high school. Like Nigeria, these countries were relatively poor during the 1960s and had an abundance of cheap labour. They could leverage this combination into a cheap yet productive workforce with educational reform.

According to the IMF (1991), education, as human capital accumulation, has played a critical role in the four Asian countries and is responsible for their incredible growth. Economies committed to education and training usually made great strides in human development and economic growth. Therefore, education is considered the means through which economic growth is achieved.

Government intervention in these countries' education did have major effects. The government directed students towards more technical and vocational studies at the beginning of industrialisation. For instance, Hong Kong's government in 1975 declared that 40% of their young should have attended technical or vocational schools. Similarly, the Singapore government also sustained technical school attendance by improving parents' and employers' attitudes. The strong support of the technical and vocational schools reduced the space for university enrolment at the beginning of industrialisation. For example, the enrolment rates in university and other tertiary education were only 6%, 10% and 5% in South Korea, Singapore and Hong Kong, respectively.

How to improve Nigeria's Education

Nigeria can improve its education system by combining short-term and long-term solutions.

Increasing government funding: One of the short-term solutions to improve education in Nigeria is to increase government funding for education. In the 2022 budget, Nigeria spent N1.29 trillion, amounting to 7.9%, on education. This falls short of the United Nations Educational, Scientific and Cultural Organisation (UNESCO) benchmark of 15 to 20% of the annual budget which the president recently committed to achieving. Nigeria should allocate a larger portion of the national budget to education to provide resources for schools, teachers, and students.

Improving teacher quality: Nigeria can also improve its education system by improving the quality of teachers. This can be done by providing teacher training and professional development opportunities and by implementing policies that attract and retain the best teachers.

Increasing access to education: Nigeria can also improve its education system by increasing access to education, particularly for children in rural and underserved areas. This can be done by building new schools, offering school meals and providing scholarships and other financial aid for students who might not otherwise be able to afford an education.

Curriculum reform: Another way to improve education in Nigeria is to reform the curriculum to make it more relevant to the needs of students and the country. This can be done by including more practical skills and real-world applications in the curriculum and by ensuring that the curriculum is aligned with the latest research and best practices in education.

Technology integration: Nigeria can also improve its education system by integrating technology into the classroom. This can be done by providing access to computers and the internet and training teachers to use technology to support learning.

Encourage private sector participation: The government can also improve education in Nigeria by encouraging private sector participation in the education sector. This can be done by providing incentives for private companies to invest in education, such as tax breaks or subsidies.

In conclusion, Nigeria can improve its education system by increasing government funding, improving teacher quality, increasing access to education, reforming the curriculum, integrating technology into the classroom, encouraging private sector participation, and addressing corruption. With the right policies and investments, Nigeria can improve its education system and drive its growth and development in the future

8.5. INFRASTRUCTURE

With Nigeria's population growing at a rate of over 2.5% per annum and an expected population of 400 million people by 2050, the current state of infrastructure in the country will likely be overwhelmed soon. Some salient infrastructure challenges in the country include insufficient road networks linking commercial centres nationwide.

Nigeria's publicly owned and operated transportation infrastructure is a major constraint to economic development. The principal ports are Lagos (Apapa and Tin Can Island), Port Harcourt, and Calabar. Of the 50,000 kilometres of roads, only a little more than 10,000 are paved, and many of these paved roads are in poor condition. In 2020 the government approved 35.944 billion nairas ($87 million) in funding for the construction and rehabilitation of major roads. Only five of Nigeria's twenty-two airports—Lagos, Kano, Port Harcourt, Enugu, and Abuja—currently receive international commercial flights. Nigeria's railway currently has eight lines that are slightly more than 2,000 miles long collectively. These railways require major rehabilitation, modernization, and expansion. It has been estimated that $3 trillion is needed to reduce Nigeria's infrastructure deficit gap over the next three decades.

Lagos State recently commissioned the construction of the Lagos Rail Mass Transit Blue Line with its own resources. The Blue Line will run 27 kilometres (17 mi) from Okokomaiko to Lagos Marina, with 13 stations and an end-to-end journey time of 35 minutes.

The Blue Line in Lagos

The largest deep seaport in West Africa is being built in Lagos via a partnership between Tolaram Group, the Lagos state government, and the National Investment Promotion Commission (NIPC). The project is expected to cost $1.5 billion with a 16.5-meter water depth capable of berthing large vessels that cannot berth in other West African waters. This will increase the efficiency of ports in the country as higher numbers of goods can be imported and exported due to the larger capacity of the port.

8.6. ELECTRICITY AND POWER IN NIGERIA

The country is home to over 200 million people, making it the most populous country in Africa, and as such, the electricity demand is significant. However, despite having vast natural resources, including oil, gas, and hydroelectricity, Nigeria has struggled to provide its citizens with a reliable and consistent electricity supply.

The country's electricity grid is old and inefficient, with frequent outages and blackouts. The transmission and distribution infrastructure is often in disrepair, leading to a significant loss of electricity during transmission. Furthermore, the grid is not well connected, with significant regional disparities in electricity supply.

According to the World Bank Statista, Nigeria ranked 171 out of 190 countries in terms of access to electricity in 2020. Only about 57% of Nigerians had access to grid electricity, while 43% or about 85 million people, lacked access. This makes Nigeria the country with the largest energy access deficit in the world.

Nigeria's power supply is notoriously epileptic and those connected to the grid endure incessant brownouts and blackouts. The lack of reliable power is a major constraint for citizens and businesses, resulting in annual economic losses estimated at $26.2 billion (₦10.1 trillion) which is equivalent to about 2% of GDP.

These challenges have made it difficult for Nigeria to meet the growing demand for electricity, which is rising by approximately 12% annually.

Despite being a significant oil and gas producer, Nigeria has not been able to translate these natural resources into a reliable electricity supply. The country's power sector is heavily subsidised and has not been able to attract significant private investment. The government has attempted to address this by privatizing the power sector, but the process has not made lots of difference, and there has been a lack of transparency in the privatization process.

The country is also part of the Economic Community of West African States and part of the West African Power Pool (WAPP), a specialized agency of ECOWAS that includes 14 of the 15 countries in the regional economic community. Nigeria currently supplies electricity to the Republic of Benin, Togo, and Niger.

The Nigerian power sector will require as much as $100 billion in investment over the next 20 years to achieve a reliable power supply.

Corruption has been a major issue in the country for decades, and the power sector has not been immune to this problem. There have been allegations of bribery, fraud, and embezzlement in the sector, which have hindered efforts to improve the reliability of the electricity supply.

Despite these challenges, there have been efforts to improve Nigeria's power sector. The government has invested in constructing new power plants and transmission infrastructure to increase the country's generating capacity. There has also been an emphasis on renewable energy, with projects such as the 10 MW Katsina Wind Farm and the 1.2 MW Solar Hybrid

Project in Kano state. These initiatives are part of the government's aim to generate at least 30% of the country's electricity from renewable sources by 2030.

The Renewable Energy Master Plan was launched in 2011 and was aimed at increasing the share of renewable energy in the country's energy mix by at least 13% by 2015, 23% by 2025, and 36% by 2030.

Solar: Nigeria is estimated to have about 427 GW of solar power potential, although its current generation capacity is estimated at 5GW.

Hydro: Nigeria is estimated to have a total large-scale hydropower potential of over 14,120 MW, producing 50,832 GW of electricity annually. The potential for small hydropower is estimated at 3,500 MW, of which only 60.58 MW (about 1.7%) has been developed. The country's hydroelectric energy is about 20% of the installed capacity.

Wind: Nigeria has great potential for onshore wind power generation. A100 MW wind power project is already under development, while offshore wind resources are being evaluated and mapped out.

Coal: Nigeria is estimated to have coal reserves of up to two billion metric tons and is exploring coal-fired electrical power as an additional power source. GON plans to expand generation by about 11,000 MW by adding six coal-fired power and nine gas plants by 2037.

How Nigeria can improve its power and electricity supply

Nigeria can improve its power and electricity supply by implementing short-term and long-term solutions.

Short-term solutions: One short-term solution to improve Nigeria's power and electricity supply is to increase electricity generation from existing power plants. This can be done by repairing and upgrading existing plants and increasing the use of natural gas as a fuel source.

Diversifying energy mix: Nigeria can also improve its power and electricity supply by diversifying its energy mix. Increasing the use of renewable energy sources, such as solar and wind power, reduces the country's reliance on fossil fuels.

Improving transmission and distribution infrastructure: Improving transmission and distribution infrastructure is another key way to improve power and electricity supply in Nigeria. By upgrading and expanding the transmission and distribution networks, the capacity and reliability of the power grid will increase.

Public-private partnership: Nigeria can also improve power and electricity supply by encouraging public-private partnerships. This can be done by incentivising private companies to invest in the power sector through tax breaks or guarantees for power purchase agreements.

Increasing access to electricity in rural areas: The government can also improve power and electricity supply by increasing access to electricity in rural areas. This can be done by providing subsidies or funding for installing solar panels and other renewable energy systems in rural communities.

Increasing energy efficiency: Another way to improve power and electricity supply in Nigeria is by increasing energy efficiency. This can be done by promoting energy-efficient appliances and practices and implementing policies that encourage energy conservation.

Addressing the issue of power theft and non-payment of bills. Power theft and non-payment of bills are major issues in Nigeria and addressing these issues can help increase the power sector's efficiency and effectiveness. This can be done by increasing enforcement of laws and regulations related to power theft and non-payment of bills, and by implementing measures to improve billing and collection systems.

Investing in research and development to develop new and innovative technologies to increase the efficiency and effectiveness of the power sector. This can be done by investing in research and development to develop new and innovative technologies, such as smart grid systems, that can help to increase the efficiency and effectiveness of the power sector.

In conclusion, Nigeria can improve its power and electricity supply by addressing corruption and mismanagement, addressing the issue of power theft and non-payment of bills, implementing policies to encourage energy conservation and energy efficiency, providing incentives for businesses and individuals to invest in renewable energy sources, and investing in research and development to develop new and innovative technologies. With the right policies and investments, Nigeria can improve its power and electricity supply and drive its growth and development in the future.

8.7. THE ROLE OF SOLAR POWER IN NIGERIA

According to Statista, the solar energy capacity in Nigeria amounted to around 33 megawatts in 2021, which increased from 15 megawatts in 2012. This is a small fraction of Nigeria's total electricity generation capacity of about 13,000 megawatts, of which only about 4,000 megawatts are available on average.

According to InfoGuide Nigeria, solar energy is a better alternative for electricity generation in Nigeria as it supersedes the current electricity source. Solar energy is abundant, renewable, clean and cost-effective in the long run. It can also provide off-grid solutions for rural areas lacking national grid access.

According to Solar Financed Africa, Nigeria has tremendous solar energy potential as Africa's largest economy and one of the sunniest countries in the world. Nigeria gets five to seven hours of sunlight daily, depending on the region. However, Nigeria faces many challenges that hinder the development of its solar energy sector, such as lack of financing, policy inconsistency, infrastructure gaps and low awareness.

According to Nigerian Price, various types and brands of solar panels are available in Nigeria at different prices and capacities. Some of the popular brands include Su-Kam, Crown Micro, Rubitec and Sunshine. The prices range from N18,000 for an 80W monocrystalline panel to N95,000 for a 350W monocrystalline panel.

Solar power can play a significant role in Nigeria's energy mix and help improve the country's power and electricity supply.

Abundant sunlight: Nigeria has abundant sunlight, making it an ideal location for solar power generation. The country has an average solar radiation of 5.5 kWh/m2 per day, which is higher than many other countries worldwide.

Cost-effective: Solar power is a cost-effective source of energy in Nigeria. The cost of solar power has dropped significantly in recent years, making it a viable option for Nigeria's energy mix.

Access to rural areas: Solar power can also help to increase access to electricity in rural areas of Nigeria. Solar panels are relatively simple to install and maintain, making them a viable option for remote communities that may not be connected to the main power grid.

Decentralized power generation: Solar power can also provide a decentralized source of power generation. This means that power can be generated locally, reducing the cost of transmission and distribution.

Environmental benefits: Solar power is a clean and renewable energy source, which can help reduce Nigeria's carbon footprint and improve the country's environmental sustainability.

Job creation: Developing a solar power industry in Nigeria can also create manufacturing, installation, and maintenance jobs.

Improving Power supply: Solar power can be a reliable source of power during the day and can help to improve the overall power supply in Nigeria.

In conclusion, solar power can play a significant role in Nigeria's energy mix, helping the country to improve its power and electricity supply. Nigeria's abundant sunlight, cost-effectiveness, and ability to access rural areas make it a viable option for its energy mix. Additionally, solar power can provide a decentralized source of power generation, create jobs, reduce the carbon footprint, and improve the overall power supply in Nigeria. With the right policies and investments, Nigeria can develop a robust solar power industry and harness this clean and renewable energy source's potential to drive future growth and development.

9. Nigeria's Macro Economics

Strengths:

11. **Rich Natural Resources**: Nigeria is rich in a range of natural resources, including crude oil, natural gas, and solid minerals, which are in high demand globally. The country's abundant resources have driven its economic growth, providing employment and generating revenue for the government.

12. **Growing Population**: Nigeria has a large and rapidly growing population, which provides a ready market for goods and services and a large pool of labour for the country's industries. The country's young and dynamic population is a key asset and has the potential to drive economic growth for years to come.

13. **Strong Agricultural Sector**: Nigeria has a large and diverse agricultural sector, producing a range of crops and livestock products in high demand domestically and internationally. The agricultural sector is an important contributor to the country's economy, providing employment and generating revenue.

14. **Robust Manufacturing Sector:** Nigeria has a growing manufacturing sector, producing a range of goods, including textiles, clothing, automobiles, and consumer goods. The manufacturing sector is an important contributor to the country's economy, providing employment and generating revenue.

Weaknesses:

1. **Dependence on Oil:** Despite its rich resources, Nigeria heavily depends on crude oil exports, which account for over 90% of its total exports. This dependence has led to a lack of economic diversification and has made it vulnerable to fluctuations in the global oil market.

2. **Corruption and Poor Governance**: Corruption is a major problem in Nigeria and negatively impacts the country's economy. The government and other stakeholders must work to tackle corruption and improve governance to create a more favourable environment for economic growth.

3. **Inadequate Infrastructure:** Nigeria's infrastructure is inadequate, with a lack of access to electricity, water, and transportation limiting economic growth and development. The government must invest in infrastructure to create a more favourable environment for business and industry.

4. **Unemployment and Poverty:** Despite its economic growth, Nigeria faces significant challenges in unemployment and poverty. The government must create jobs and reduce poverty to ensure that all citizens benefit from economic growth.

5. **Inequality:** Nigeria has a high level of income inequality, with the rich getting richer and the poor getting poorer. This has resulted in widespread poverty, with millions of Nigerians living in extreme poverty and struggling to access basic needs such as food, shelter, and healthcare.

6. **Inflation:** Nigeria has faced high levels of inflation in recent years, resulting in rising food and fuel prices and making it difficult for ordinary Nigerians to make ends meet.

Challenges

Nigeria is the largest economy in Africa, but despite its economic growth, the country continues to face significant economic and political challenges that significantly impact ordinary Nigerians' lives.

1. **Politics** in Nigeria is also a significant challenge. The country has a history of political instability, and the current government has been criticized for handling corruption and human rights issues, including ongoing security challenges, like the fight against Boko Haram in the northeast and conflicts with militant groups in the Niger Delta region. Nigeria's biggest security challenge is the ongoing Boko Haram insurgency in the northeast. This violent extremist group has carried out a campaign of terror, including bombings, assassinations, and kidnappings, and has resulted in widespread displacement, poverty, and loss of life. The Nigerian government has been working to defeat Boko Haram, but the group continues threatening the country's security.

2. **Unemployment**: Despite its economic growth, Nigeria continues to face high levels of unemployment, particularly among young people. This has resulted in poverty, social unrest, and increased crime and has devastated the lives of ordinary Nigerians.

3. **Kidnapping and Banditry**: Kidnapping and banditry are also major security challenges in Nigeria, particularly in the northern and central regions of the country. This has resulted in widespread fear and insecurity and has made it difficult for ordinary Nigerians to go about their daily lives.

4. **Ethnic and Religious Conflict**: Nigeria is diverse, with over 500 ethnic groups and over 1,000 languages. This

diversity has often been a source of strength for the country but has also led to tensions between ethnic and religious groups. This has resulted in sporadic outbreaks of ethnic and religious violence and has negatively impacted the country's stability and security.

5. **Cybercrime**: Nigeria is also facing a growing threat from cybercrime, including online fraud, hacking, and cyber-attacks. This has had a negative impact on the economy, as well as on individual citizens, who are often targeted by cybercriminals.

6. **The country's human rights record** has also been a source of concern. There have been reports of human rights abuses by security forces and the government has been criticized for its handling of protests and civil society activism.

7. **Healthcare:** Nigeria's healthcare system is facing numerous challenges, including a shortage of healthcare providers, inadequate funding, and inadequate infrastructure. On the other hand, the country is also experiencing growth in the healthcare sector, with a growing number of private hospitals and clinics and a growing demand for healthcare services. This presents opportunities for investment and innovation in the healthcare sector and for developing new and improved healthcare services.

8. **Education**: Education is another critical area where Nigeria faces both challenges and opportunities. The country is facing a shortage of qualified teachers, inadequate funding for education, and a lack of access to quality education for many Nigerians. On the other hand, the country is also experiencing growth in the education sector, with an increasing number of private

schools and universities and a growing market for education services. This presents opportunities for investment and innovation in the education sector and for developing new and improved educational services.

9. **Infrastructure:** Finally, infrastructure is another important area where Nigeria faces both challenges and opportunities. The country is facing a shortage of basic infrastructure, such as roads, bridges, and power supplies, as well as a lack of investment in new infrastructure projects. On the other hand, the country is also experiencing growth in the infrastructure sector, with new projects underway and a growing market for infrastructure services. This presents opportunities for investment and innovation in the infrastructure sector and for developing new and improved infrastructure services.

In conclusion, Nigeria is a country that is facing numerous challenges and opportunities in the fields of healthcare, education, and infrastructure. Addressing these challenges and seizing these opportunities will require strategic planning, investment, and collaboration between the government, the private sector, and other stakeholders. With its rich history, diverse culture, and growing economy, Nigeria has the potential to become a leader in these fields, but this will require careful management of its resources and strategic investment in its people, education, and infrastructure. By working together, Nigeria can build a strong and vibrant future for all its citizens.

9.1. THE SOLUTION TO NIGERIA'S CHALLENGES

Solving the challenges facing Nigeria will require a multifaceted approach that addresses the root causes of these issues. Some possible solutions to Nigeria's challenges include:

Combating corruption: One of Nigeria's main challenges is corruption, which undermines the country's economy and hinders its development. To combat corruption, Nigeria needs to strengthen its institutions and laws to ensure that those who engage in corrupt activities are held accountable. This can be done through increased transparency, oversight, and improved access to information.

Improving governance: Good governance is crucial for addressing the challenges facing Nigeria. This includes strengthening the rule of law, promoting accountability and transparency, and improving the delivery of public services. This can be achieved by implementing effective policies, such as the use of technology for e-governance and the participation of citizens in decision-making processes.

Investing in education: Education is key to addressing many challenges facing Nigeria. By investing in education, the country can provide its citizens with the skills and knowledge they need to compete in the global economy and become active, engaged citizens. This can be done through funding for schools, scholarships, and other educational programs.

Promoting economic development: Economic development is essential for addressing Nigeria's challenges. This can be achieved through policies that promote entrepreneurship, attract investment, and create jobs. This can be done through the development of infrastructure, the provision of financial services, and the promotion of trade and investment.

Tackling poverty: Poverty is a major challenge facing Nigeria and a root cause of many of the other issues the country faces. To tackle poverty, Nigeria must implement policies promoting economic growth, reducing inequality, and improving access to basic services, such as health and education.

Improving security: Nigeria is facing security challenges that need to be addressed. This can be done through the development of effective security policies, the training of security forces, and the improvement of intelligence-gathering capabilities.

Encouraging the youth: As previously discussed, the youths constitute a large proportion of the population and have the potential to drive the country's development through their talents, skills and innovative ideas. Empowering and investing in the youth is crucial for addressing Nigeria's challenges.

Promoting peace and stability: Peace and stability are crucial for addressing Nigeria's challenges. This can be achieved through the promotion of peaceful coexistence and tolerance among the different ethnic and religious groups in the country.

In conclusion, addressing NigeriaNigeria's challenges will require a multifaceted approach to addressing the root causes of these issues. By implementing effective policies and programs, Nigeria can overcome these challenges and continue to grow and prosper.

10. Nigeria's Tech Startup Ecosystem

Nigeria joined the tech startup scene in Africa relatively later than countries such as South Africa, Kenya, and Egypt. However, what Nigeria lost in time was gained in the pace with which the local startup ecosystem has grown over the last decade.

In 2012, two Harvard Business School graduates from Nigeria co-founded Jumia, a Nigerian e-commerce hub and one of the first tech start-ups in the country. Since then, several Nigerian diasporas returning home have established more startup companies, such as IrokoTV, Flutterwave, and Bamboo, which employ several thousand Nigerians.

In 2018, Nigeria gained significant funding from Andela ($40M), Flutterwave ($ 10M), Terragon Group ($5M), Cars45 ($5M), Resource ($3.5M), Paystack ($1.3M). This level of funding shows investors' confidence in the feasibility and viability of the ecosystem.

In 2019, COVID-19 caused oil prices to fall to as low as $20 per barrel for oil-producing countries like Nigeria. In the same year, the technology industry received a substantial financial boost as the stay-at-home order (lockdown) worldwide had a positive spill-back effect on digital adoption and the use of technology for financial services, especially in Sub-Saharan African countries. According to the WeeTracker report, African tech startups generated $1.34 billion in 2019. Nigeria attracted the most significant funding compared to other countries.

Nigeria went from attracting 24% of the $185 million funding raised by African tech startups in 2015 to 50.5%, becoming the most sought-after tech investment destination in Sub-Saharan Africa. Nigerian-focused startups; Interswitch, OPay ($50M), Andela, Palmpay, accounted for most of the top venture deals on the continent in 2019. New startups emerging out of Nigeria remain the favourites of venture capitalists ready to invest heavily. Startups like Kobo 360 ($30M), Team apt ($5M), Farmcrowdy ($2M), Kudi ($5M), and MAX (Metro Africa Express) ($7M).

This growth has positioned Nigeria as the largest tech market on the African continent, with 90 tech hubs and a growing and vibrant customer base, many of which have become household names. With 200 million people (72% of the population) now having mobile telephone access, internet penetration is projected to reach 85.3% in 2025, up from under 2% in 2001. The world's largest tech giants—IBM, Microsoft, Google, and CISCO—have presences in the country. Jobberman estimates the sector will add $88 billion to the economy by 2027.

Nigeria's ICT sector has grown from less than 1% of GDP in 2001 to almost 10% in 2018 and over 15% in 2020, surpassing South Africa to emerge as a premier investment destination.

In Nigeria, the ICT industry contributed 14.07% and 17.83% to the country's GDP in the first and second quarters of 2022. This was when the oil sector only contributed an average of 9.2% to GDP.

Financing, lending, payments, and remittances currently account for 69% of Nigeria's Fintech landscape, leaving 31% to relatively untapped categories such as crowd computing, big data, business solutions, insurance, and wealth management. This industry has the potential to create value and solve some of the age-long problems of Nigeria through technological innovation and inventions.

The coming of age of Generation Z to the job market and maturing of the Nigerian ecosystem will seal Nigeria's fate to its next future.

11. Nigerian Contributions to the World

Nigeria has made many contributions to the world in various fields such as politics, science, culture, sports, literature, and more.

Field of education. Nigeria has a long history of education and has a large number of universities, colleges and research institutes. Nigeria has 49 Federal Universities, 54 State Universities and 99 Private Universities. Nigeria has seen a booming middle and elite class who value quality education, have international exposure, specific educational preferences, a higher disposable income, and general affluence — some of which drive the thirst for international education.

Nigeria currently ranks 10th on the International Student Leading Place of Origin. Nigerians in America have made significant contributions to education. Many have become professors, researchers, and educators in various universities across the United States and have helped promote knowledge advancement in various fields. Nigerians in the United States constitute one of the largest and most educated groups of African immigrants. According to data from the United States Census Bureau, Nigerian immigrants in the United States are among the most educated groups of African immigrants. According to data from the Migration Policy Institute, about 50% of Nigerian immigrants in the United States have at least a bachelor's degree, compared to 30% of all immigrants in the United States. They have made significant contributions to the field of education as professors, researchers, and educators in various universities across the United States.

Literature: Nigeria has a rich literary tradition, and Nigerian authors have made significant contributions to the world of literature. Some notable Nigerian authors include Chinua Achebe, Wole Soyinka, Chimamanda Ngozi Adichie, and Ben Okri, who have written books widely read and critically acclaimed worldwide. These authors have contributed to promoting Nigerian culture and helped shape the world's understanding of Africa and the African experience.

Biotechnology: Nigeria has a thriving biotechnology sector, and its scientists are making important contributions to the global understanding of diseases and health conditions. Nigerian researchers have developed innovative infectious disease control, vaccine development, and cancer research solutions. For example, scientists at the University of Nigeria have developed a new vaccine that can be used to treat tuberculosis.

Space Science: Nigeria has also made important contributions to the field of space science, with the country's space program playing a key role in advancing the country's technological capabilities. Nigerian scientists have developed a range of satellites, including remote sensing and communication satellites, which have been used to monitor weather patterns, support disaster response efforts, and provide telecommunications services. These satellites have significantly impacted the country's ability to respond to natural disasters and support economic development.

Field of diplomacy. Nigeria is one of Africa's most influential nations and has played a critical role in shaping the continent's political and diplomatic landscape. The country has played an important role in resolving conflicts in Africa and has served as a mediator in several peace negotiations. Nigerian peacekeepers have also been deployed to various peacekeeping missions around the world. The country is an active member of the United Nations and other international organizations. The country has provided troops and resources to peacekeeping missions in Sierra Leone, Liberia, and Darfur countries. Nigerian peacekeepers have played a key role in supporting the stability of these countries. Nigerian diplomats have also been instrumental in mediating peace negotiations and helping to resolve conflicts in several African countries, including the Democratic Republic of Congo and South Sudan.

Nigeria's contributions to the world of religion. The country is simultaneously home to some of the world's largest Christian and Muslim populations. Nigeria is divided roughly in half between Muslims living mostly in the north and Christians in the south. Indigenous religions, such as those native to the Igbo and Yoruba ethnicities, are in the minority. Nigeria has been a centre of Christian activity and growth. Nigerian

Christians and Muslims have also made significant contributions to the development of theological education and mission work, and they have inspired countless people worldwide to embrace the Christian faith. Some notable Nigerian religious leaders include David Oyedepo, Enoch Adeboye, and Matthew Ashimolowo, who have played an important role in promoting Christianity in Nigeria.

Nigeria is also home to a rich tradition of indigenous African religions, and the country has made significant contributions to preserving and promoting these ancient spiritual practices.

Nigerian role in the global economy — Nigeria plays a significant role in the global economy as the largest economy in Africa and a member of the G20 group of nations. As the largest economy in Africa, Nigeria has played a key role in representing the continent's interests within the G20. Through its participation in the G20, Nigeria has been able to voice the concerns of African countries and promote the importance of addressing issues such as poverty, inequality, and sustainable development. Nigeria has also played an active role in promoting trade and investment opportunities in Africa, and its contributions to the G20 have helped to raise the continent's profile on the global stage.

Nigeria is also an important player in the agricultural sector, which is a major employer and contributor to the country's GDP. The country is one of the world's largest producers of palm oil, rubber, and cocoa and is also a major producer of other agricultural products, such as groundnuts, yams, and cassava. The agricultural sector has the potential to play a significant role in the country's economic development and in reducing poverty.

Film and Television: Nigeria has become a significant player in the film and television industry with a thriving movie industry known as Nollywood. The industry produces over 2,000 films each year and has become one of the largest film industries in the world, after Hollywood and Bollywood. Nigerian filmmakers have explored various themes and subjects, from traditional folklore and contemporary social issues to romance and action. Nigerian television dramas and soap operas are also popular across Africa, showcasing the country's unique storytelling abilities.

Music: Nigeria has a rich musical heritage, and its music has profoundly impacted the entertainment world. Nigerian musicians have blended traditional African rhythms with contemporary styles to create a unique sound that has captured the hearts of audiences worldwide. Nigerian music is characterized by its high energy, powerful vocals, and infectious beats, and it has inspired many other musical genres, including Afrobeats, which has become a global phenomenon. Nigerian artists such as Fela Anikulapo, Sunny Ade, Burna Boy, Wizkid, and Davido have become international superstars, taking the Nigerian music scene to new heights and introducing the world to the country's vibrant musical heritage.

Dance: Nigerian dance has also significantly impacted the entertainment world, with traditional styles such as the high-energy "Shaku Shaku" and "Zanku" becoming popular worldwide. Nigerian dance has been incorporated into many different musical genres and has inspired the creation of new dance styles, such as "Afrobeats Dance." Nigerian dancers are known for their high-energy performances and captivating stage presence, and their influence has been felt in various dance styles, from hip-hop to contemporary dance.

Festac 77, the first Festac event, was the largest cultural gathering in Africa;it was attended by dignitaries, artists and performers from around the world. The event was a major success, putting Nigeria on the map as a cultural destination. The festival featured a wide range of cultural activities such as music, dance, theatre, art, and film. It also included an exhibition of traditional and contemporary art from Nigeria and other African countries. The festival has played an important role in promoting a positive image of Nigeria and its cultural heritage, and it has helped to promote understanding and appreciation of Nigerian culture on a global scale.

Festac 77

Sports: Nigeria has produced world-class athletes who have competed at the highest levels and made significant contributions to the world of sports. Football is undoubtedly one of the most popular sports in Nigeria, and the country has produced some of the best footballers in the world. From the legendary Jay-Jay Okocha, Mikel Obi, Kanu Nwankwo to current stars like Bukayo Saka, Nigerian footballers have thrilled audiences with their skill and flair. They have represented the country with distinction on the international stage. Nigeria has produced several world-class sprinters, including Blessing Okagbere, Chioma Ajunwa, and Tobi Amusan, who broke the 100 metres hurdles world record in 2022. Nigeria is also a force to be reckoned with in the boxing world as the country has produced several world-class fighters. From Bash Ali, who held several world titles in the 1980s and 90s, to current stars like Anthony Joshua, Nigerian boxers have made their mark in the sport. Nigeria has produced several talented players who have significantly impacted the sport, from Michael Eric, who played in the NBA and Europe, to current stars, like Al-Farouq Aminu.

Fashion: Nigeria has a rich tradition of intricate textiles and unique fashion styles, and its fashion industry has gained worldwide recognition. Nigerian fashion designers have drawn on traditional styles and materials to create modern, innovative designs showcased at international fashion events. The country's vibrant fashion scene has inspired a new generation of designers who are creating fashion lines that are both stylish and sustainable.

Research and Innovation: Nigeria has a growing community of researchers and innovators who are working to solve some of the country's most pressing challenges. Scientists and engineers in Nigeria have developed innovative solutions in fields such as renewable energy, healthcare, and agriculture. For example, researchers at the University of Nigeria have developed low-cost solar panels that can be used in rural areas to provide clean energy. Similarly, Nigerian entrepreneurs have developed mobile health platforms that make healthcare services more accessible to rural communities. These contributions demonstrate Nigeria's commitment to using science and technology to address the country's most pressing challenges.

Regional Integration: Nigeria has been a driving force behind regional integration in Africa, and the country has been instrumental in promoting greater cooperation and collaboration among African nations. Nigeria has worked to promote economic integration, political stability, and peace on the continent through its leadership in organizations such as the African Union and the Economic Community of West African States (ECOWAS). Nigeria has also been a strong advocate for African nations working together to address shared challenges, such as climate change and economic development.

11.1. NOTABLE NIGERIANS IN ART, SCIENCE AND TECHNOLOGY

Nigeria has produced several notable scientists and technology professionals who have made significant contributions to their fields. These individuals have made pioneering contributions in computer science, literature, medicine, virology, physics, renewable energy and many more. They have helped promote a positive image of Nigeria and its scientific and technological capabilities on a global scale. Some notable Nigerians in science and technology include:

Dr. Phillip Emeagwali: A computer scientist and engineer, Dr. Emeagwali is best known for his work in the field of high-performance computing. He is credited with developing the world's first computer program to perform a billion calculations per second, and his work has been instrumental in developing supercomputers. Dr. Emeagwali is also known for his contributions to the field of parallel processing and distributed computing.

Dr. Phillip EmeagwaliIweala   Dr. Ngozi Okonjo-Iweala

Dr. Ngozi Okonjo-Iweala is an economist and former finance minister of Nigeria. She is the first woman and the first African to hold the position of Director-General of the World Trade Organization. Dr. Okonjo-Iweala has also served as a managing director at the World Bank and has held various senior positions in the Nigerian government.

Dr. Chinua Achebe: A world-renowned novelist, Dr. Chinua Achebe is also a notable figure in the field of literature and has written many books on the African experience and contributed to promoting African culture. His books, including "Things Fall Apart", have been translated into over 50 languages and have sold millions of copies worldwide. He is also a cultural ambassador and has helped to promote a positive image of Nigeria and Africa through his work.

Dr. Oyewale Tomori: A virologist and medical researcher, is best known for his work in tropical medicine and his contributions to understanding diseases such as Lassa fever and yellow fever.

Dr. Julius Atete: A renowned physicist, is best known for his contributions to the field of solar energy and for his work in the design and development of solar cells and solar-powered systems. He made significant contributions to developing sustainable energy solutions in Nigeria and Africa.

Professor Abiodun AlaoDosunmu   Bayo

Professor Abiodun Alao, a professor of African Studies. The first black African to attain a professorial cadre at King's College, University of London, and the first black African scholar to deliver an inaugural lecture since the institution was established in 1829.

Bayo Dosunmu, Chief Executive, Lambeth London Borough Council and one of the 32 in the United Kingdom capital of London.

Dr. Clement Adebamowo, a medical researcher who has made significant contributions to the understanding of cancer epidemiology and health disparities in Africa

Dr Adenike Osofisan is a chemist and materials scientist who has made significant contributions to the field of biomaterials and drug delivery systems.

Dr Oluyinka Olutoye is a renowned pediatric surgeon who has made pioneering contributions in fetal surgery.

Dr Ndubuisi Ekekwe, an engineer and entrepreneur who has made significant contributions to the field of microelectronics and has founded several companies that are helping to drive technological innovation in Nigeria.

Dr. Chuka Onwuchekwa is a renowned engineer, inventor and entrepreneur; Dr. Onwuchekwa is the founder and CEO of two successful engineering companies in the United States. He is also the inventor of several patented technologies and has been recognized for his contributions to the field of engineering.

Dr. Christopher Kolade is a former Nigerian High commissioner to the United Kingdom and former chairman of Cadbury Nigeria Plc. He is also a business consultant and management expert.

Adebayo Ogunlesi is a renowned investment banker and business magnate. He is the founder and chairman of Global Infrastructure Partners (GIP), one of the world's largest infrastructure investment funds. Ogunlesi has served on the board of several major companies, including Goldman Sachs and American International Group (AIG).

Mo Abudu is a media entrepreneur. She is the founder and CEO of EbonyLife TV, the first African global black entertainment and lifestyle network. She is also the creator and executive producer of several successful TV shows and films, including "The Governor" and "Fifty."

Dr Oluyinka Olutoye is a renowned pediatric surgeon and professor at Texas Children's Hospital and Baylor College of Medicine. He is known for performing ground-breaking surgeries on babies still in the womb and has been recognized for his contributions to pediatric surgery.

Dr Bennet Omalu is a forensic pathologist and neuropathologist known for his discovery of chronic traumatic encephalopathy (CTE) in American football players. He is the subject of the 2015 film "Concussion" starring Will Smith and has been recognized for his contributions to medicine and sports science.

Dr Okey Onyejekwe is a renowned economist. He is a professor of economics at the University of Texas at Austin and a senior fellow at the United Nations Economic Commission for Africa.

Chika Okeke-Agulu is a renowned art historian. He is a professor of art history at Princeton University and an expert on the art and culture of Africa.

Ndidi Nwuneli is a renowned social entrepreneur. She is the founder of LEAP Africa, a non-profit organization that promotes leadership and entrepreneurship in Africa. Nwuneli is a recognized expert on leadership, entrepreneurship, and social innovation and has received several awards and recognitions for her contributions in these fields.

Oluseyi Dasilva is a renowned entrepreneur and technology expert. He is the co-founder and CEO of Interswitch, Africa's leading digital payments and commerce company.

Dr Olufunmilayo Olopade is a renowned physician and researcher. She is a professor of medicine and human genetics at the University of Chicago and an expert in the field of breast cancer research.

Dr Funmi Osibodu is a renowned chemist. She is a professor of chemistry at the University of California, Los Angeles and an expert in materials science and nanotechnology.

Dr Funmi Quadri is a renowned mathematician. She is a professor of mathematics at the University of California, Berkeley and an expert in the field of algebraic geometry.

11.2. CONTRIBUTION OF THE NIGERIANS' DIASPORA

Millions of Nigerians live in a diaspora. The mass migration of Nigerians started during the transatlantic slave trade that stretched between 1400–1900. During this period alone, more than a third, 5.5m of the ten million people transported as slaves to the Americas from Africa were Nigerians.

There was also another modern mass migration from Nigeria which started just before independence. In the 1960s, the higher education policies of newly independent Nigeria reflected a need for the country to train its elites to take on the senior position left by the British. The Southwest and Southeast of Nigeria concluded that education was the answer, and these two regions embarked on universal primary education, making education free and accessible for all. The regions even went as far as sponsoring and educating their students abroad in Britain. They offered scholarships to potential students and expected them to return home to contribute their newly acquired skills and knowledge to their country's development.

However, since the 1980s, the inspiration for emigration from Nigeria has been based heavily on socio-economic issues such as warfare, insecurity, economic instability and civil unrest.

IOM define diasporas as "migrants or descendants of migrants, whose identity and sense of belonging have been shaped by their migration experience and background". "The term 'diasporas' has no set definition, and its meaning is usually based on the definition of the host countries.

The United Nations Department of Economic and Social Affairs (Desa) most recent estimate of Nigeria's diaspora in 2020 is 2 million, based on the empirical data that was received from the host country's population censuses, registers and nationally representative surveys. However, the Central Bank of Nigeria estimated more than 20 million Nigerians are in the diaspora (about 10% of the country's population).

The differences between the two estimates of the Nigerian diaspora are due to differences in definition. Many host nations only count foreign-born or foreign citizens but exclude the children and grandchildren of migrants born in the host countries. The author of this book believes that the figure from the Central Bank of Nigeria is more realistic. A Nigerian Mayor of Brent, London UK, Michael Adeyeye, estimates that the Nigerian population in London alone is over one million.

The largest Nigerian communities in the diaspora are in the United Kingdom and the United States, with about 3,000,000 and 5,000,000, respectively. Other countries that followed closely were South Africa, Gambia, Brazil and Canada.

The World Bank estimates Nigeria's annual remittances in 2022 as $ 21 billion — again, this only accounts for the transfers made through the country's formal banking system. This figure does not account for money sent by Nigerians abroad to their relatives and friends in Nigeria through some informal means without using the banks. The World Bank and the International Monetary Fund estimated that the remittances sent through informal channels could be 50% higher than those paid using official systems. That is over half of the country's foreign reserves sent in by the Nigerian diaspora in one year.

According to the United Nations, a Nigerian professional working in the United States contributes about $100,000 annually to the US economy and remits an average of $300 per month to Nigeria.

Nigerians are among the highest educated migration groups and also the most successful ethnic group in the United States. Nigerians in the diaspora have distinguished themselves as highly-educated achievers in music, medicine, business and corporate enterprise, sports, music, education, and other sectors of the diaspora economy.

Nigerians in the diaspora have achieved significant success in various communities due to personal attributes like resilience, competitiveness, hard work, resourcefulness, and so many others. Also, the level of infrastructural development in the diaspora communities, political system and culture, and efficient government policies aid their success.

12. The Future of Nigeria

Nigeria, with a population of over 200 million people, is the most populous country in Africa and one of the largest economies on the continent. Despite facing significant challenges, including political instability, corruption, and security threats, Nigeria has enormous potential for growth and development. In this chapter, we will examine the emerging opportunities and potential for political and social reform in Nigeria and its regional and global significance.

Emerging Opportunities for Growth and Development

Nigeria has significant opportunities for growth and development, particularly in agriculture, manufacturing, and technology. The agricultural sector, which employs about 70% of the population and accounts for over 20% of GDP, has the potential to drive economic growth and development. With vast arable land, abundant water resources, and a growing population, Nigeria can become a major food producer and exporter. The government's focus on agriculture and agribusiness through programs such as the Agricultural Transformation Agenda (ATA) and the Anchor Borrowers Program (ABP) has shown significant potential for growth.

In addition to agriculture, Nigeria has the potential to become a manufacturing hub in Africa. With a large consumer market, abundant natural resources, and a strategic location, Nigeria can attract foreign investment and develop its manufacturing capacity. The government's focus on industrialization through programs such as the Nigeria Industrial Revolution Plan (NIRP) and the National Automotive Industry Development Plan (NAIDP) has shown promising results.

Moreover, Nigeria's growing technology industry, often called "Naija Tech," is attracting international attention and investment. With a young and talented workforce, a growing startup ecosystem, and a large market, Nigeria can become a leading technology hub in Africa. The government's focus on digital transformation through programs such as the National Digital Economy Policy and Strategy and the NITDA Innovation and Entrepreneurship Support Scheme is a step in the right direction.

Potential for Political and Social Reform

Nigeria has significant political and social reform potential, particularly in democracy, human rights, and social justice. Despite its long-standing history of military coups, Nigeria has made significant progress in democratization since its return to civilian rule in 1999. The country has held several peaceful and credible elections which have led to the transfer of power from one civilian government to another. The 2023 general elections will determine who will succeed President Muhammadu Buhari as Nigeria's leader. The elections are expected to be highly competitive and contentious among various political parties and candidates. There are still significant challenges to democratic consolidation, including weak institutions, corruption, and electoral violence.

Moreover, Nigeria faces significant challenges in human rights and social justice, particularly in security, gender equality, and human development. The country has faced security threats, including Boko Haram insurgency in the northeast, banditry in the northwest, and separatist agitations in the southeast. The government's response to these threats has been criticized for human rights abuses, including extrajudicial killings, arbitrary arrests, and torture.

Nigeria also faces significant challenges in gender equality, with women facing significant barriers to education, health-care, and political participation. The country ranks 133 out of 189 countries in the UNDP's Gender Inequality Index, with women accounting for only 6% of parliamentarians.

Regional and Global Significance

Nigeria's regional and global significance cannot be overstated. As the most populous country in Africa and the largest econo-my on the continent, Nigeria has the potential to drive region-al integration and promote peace and stability. The country's leadership role in the Economic Community of West African States (ECOWAS) and other regional organizations has been critical in resolving conflicts and promoting economic devel-opment in the region.

Moreover, Nigeria's global significance extends beyond Africa. The country is a member of the United Nations, the Common-wealth, and the African Union and has significant diplomatic influence in the region and beyond.

Human Capital — In addition to economic growth, political and social reform, and regional and global significance, Ni-geria's future prospects also depend on the country's human capital. Nigeria has a large and growing population, which could be a significant asset for the country's future develop-ment, provided that the population is healthy, educated, and skilled. However, Nigeria faces many challenges in this area.

Nigeria's education system faces significant challenges, with low levels of funding, inadequate infrastructure, and poor teacher quality. This has resulted in low levels of literacy and numeracy among Nigeria's population, particularly in rural areas. Improving the quality and accessibility of education will be essential for Nigeria's future prosperity.

Health is another area where Nigeria faces significant challenges. The country has a high burden of disease, including infectious diseases such as malaria and HIV/AIDS, as well as non-communicable diseases, such as diabetes and cardiovascular disease. Nigeria also has one of the highest maternal mortality rates in the world. Improving access to healthcare and addressing the underlying determinants of poor health will be crucial for Nigeria's future development.

In addition to education and health, Nigeria also faces significant challenges in terms of governance and corruption. Corruption is endemic in many sectors of Nigerian society, including politics, business, and public services. Addressing corruption and improving governance will be essential for Nigeria's future development and for creating an enabling environment for businesses and investors.

Overall, Nigeria's prospects are promising, but the country faces significant challenges in various areas. Addressing these challenges will require a sustained effort by the government, civil society, and the private sector. However, suppose Nigeria can successfully address these challenges and capitalize on its many assets, including its human capital. In that case, the country has the potential to become a regional and global powerhouse in the future.

The development of its infrastructure. Nigeria currently faces significant challenges in this area, with the inadequate road, rail, and air transport systems and limited access to electricity and water. Addressing these challenges will require significant investment and improvements in the regulatory environment to attract private sector investment.

As Nigeria looks towards the future, it will be important for policymakers to take a long-term perspective and prioritize sustainable development. This will require a shift away from the country's traditional reliance on oil exports and towards more diversified and inclusive economic growth.

In addition, Nigeria will need to address the challenges posed by rapid urbanization and a growing population. This will require investments in housing, transportation, and urban infrastructure, as well as improvements in social services such as education and healthcare.

As a country vulnerable to the effects of climate change, such as rising sea levels and extreme weather events, Nigeria will need to take action to mitigate these risks and adapt to the changing climate.

Finally, Nigeria's future prospects will depend on its ability to leverage its position as a regional and global player. Nigeria is the largest economy in Africa and has significant geopolitical influence. Nigeria can become a leader in promoting regional stability and development by strengthening its regional ties and playing an active role in international organizations, such as the United Nations and the African Union.

13. Conclusion

In this book, we examined the history, politics, economy, society, and culture of Nigeria, one of Africa's largest and most diverse countries. We explored Nigeria's rich and complex past, from its pre-colonial empires to its post-independence struggles for democracy and development. We analyzed Nigeria's political system, including its federalism, ethnic diversity, and political parties. We also evaluated Nigeria's economy, including its dependence on oil, poverty, inequality, unemployment challenges, and potential for diversification and innovation. We examined Nigeria's society, including its ethnic, religious, and gender dynamics, security, education, health challenges, and potential for social inclusion and empowerment. And we celebrated Nigeria's culture, including its music, literature, film, and art, as well as its resilience, creativity, and hospitality traditions.

Throughout this book, we sought to provide a comprehensive and balanced perspective on Nigeria and how it is perceived by other Africans, drawing on a wide range of sources and viewpoints and engaging with the complex realities of Nigeria's past and present. We also sought to highlight the opportunities and challenges of Nigeria's future and offer some recommendations for how Nigeria can overcome its obstacles and realize its potential.

Nigeria has many strengths in terms of opportunities, including its large and young population, abundant natural resources, strategic location in West Africa, and vibrant culture and creativity. Nigeria can leverage these strengths to pursue a more diversified, inclusive, and sustainable development path prioritising human capital, innovation, and governance reform. Nigeria can also play a more active and constructive role in regional and global affairs, promoting peace, security, and development in West Africa and beyond.

Nigeria faces many challenges, including political instability, corruption, insecurity, poverty, inequality, and environmental degradation. Nigeria needs to address these challenges through comprehensive and coordinated reforms that strengthen democratic institutions, promote transparency and accountability, address the root causes of violence and extremism, invest in human development, and protect the environment. Nigeria must also engage with its diverse and vibrant civil society, including youth, women, and marginalized groups, and build a more inclusive and participatory political culture.

In conclusion, Nigeria is a complex and dynamic country with many opportunities and challenges. Nigeria's future depends on how it navigates these challenges and harnesses its opportunities. This book has sought to provide a comprehensive and nuanced perspective on Nigeria and offer some recommendations for how Nigeria can build a more prosperous, peaceful, and inclusive future for its people and the region. We hope this book will contribute to a better understanding of Nigeria and lead to a more constructive and collaborative engagement with Nigeria by scholars, policymakers, and citizens alike.

14. Glossary

Boko Haram is a jihadist group based in northeastern Nigeria seeking to establish an Islamic caliphate.

Colonialism — the policy of acquiring and maintaining colonies and exploiting their resources and people for the benefit of the colonizing power.

Corruption — the abuse of power for personal gain or enrichment.

Democracy — a form of government in which power is held by the people through free and fair elections.

Dictatorship — a form of government in which one person or a small group holds absolute power and authority.

Economic Growth — an increase in the production of goods and services in a country over time.

Ethnicity — a shared cultural identity or heritage of a group of people.

Federalism — a system of government in which power is shared between a central authority and constituent political units, such as states or provinces.

Foreign Direct Investment (FDI) — investment made by a foreign company in the economy of another country.

Foreign Policy — a set of strategies and principles adopted by a country to promote its interests and maintain relations with other countries.

GDP (Gross Domestic Product) — a measure of the size and health of an economy, representing the total value of goods and services produced within a country in a given period.

Gerontocracy — a form of oligarchical rule in which an entity is ruled by leaders who are significantly older than most of the adult population. In many political structures, power within the ruling class accumulates with age, making the oldest individuals the holders of the most power

Human Development Index (HDI) — a composite measure of a country's social and economic development, taking into account factors such as education, healthcare, and income.

Human Rights — fundamental rights and freedoms to which all individuals are entitled, such as the right to life, liberty, and equality before the law.

Inequality — the unequal distribution of resources and opportunities among individuals or groups in a society.

Infrastructure — the physical structures and facilities needed for the functioning of a society, such as roads, bridges, and communication networks.

Military Regime — a government led by military officers who have seized power by force.

Natural Resources — materials or substances that exist in nature and are used for economic gain.

Non-Governmental Organization (NGO) — an organization that operates independently of government and aims to address social or environmental issues.

Oil — a fossil fuel that is the primary source of Nigeria's revenue and foreign exchange earnings.

Political Instability — the absence of a stable political environment characterized by frequent changes in leadership and government.

Political Corruption — the manipulation of political institutions or processes for personal gain or the benefit of a specific group.

Poverty — a condition characterized by the lack of basic necessities and resources needed for a decent standard of living.

Regional Integration — the process of countries in a region coming together to promote economic and political cooperation.

Resource Curse — a phenomenon in which countries rich in natural resources experience negative economic and political consequences such as corruption, conflict, and lack of economic diversification.

Social Structures — the organized patterns of relationships and interactions within a society.

Sustainable Development — development that meets the needs of the present without compromising the ability of future generations to meet their own needs.

Structural Adjustment Programs (SAPs) — economic policies imposed by international financial institutions such as the World Bank and the International Monetary Fund (IMF) on developing countries in exchange for loans or debt relief in the pursuit of political aims.

Terrorism — the use of violence and intimidation

Transition to Democracy — the process of moving from a dictatorship or military regime to a democratic form of government.

Transparency — the quality of being open and honest and the degree to which information is accessible to the public.

Universal Basic Education (UBE) — a government policy that aims to provide free and compulsory education for all children up to a certain level.

UN (United Nations) — an international organization founded in 1945 to promote peace, security, and cooperation among member countries.

West Africa is a sub-region comprising 16 countries, including Nigeria, Ghana, and Senegal.

World Bank — an international financial institution that provides loans and technical assistance to developing countries for economic development projects.

Youth Unemployment — the percentage of unemployed young people, which is a major challenge in Nigeria and many other developing countries.

15. References

Adebayo, A. (2019). Nigeria: A New History of a Turbulent Century. London: Zed Books.

Adejumobi, S. (2007). The History of Ethiopia. Westport, CT: Greenwood Press.

Central Intelligence Agency, The World Factbook Africa: Nigeria. Accessed on May 28, 2022

Central Intelligence Agency. (2021). The World Factbook — Nigeria. Retrieved from https://www.cia.gov/the-world-factbook/countries/nigeria/

Collier, P., & Gunning, J. W. (1999). Why Has Africa Grown Slowly? Journal of Economic Perspectives, 13(3), 3-22.

Eke, C. C., & Ugwuanyi, C. C. (2016). Nigeria's Foreign Policy: Continuity and Change. Journal of Social and Political Sciences, 1(1), 10-23.

Forbes Global 2000 rankings, The World's Biggest Public Companies. Accessed on May 28, 2022

International Monetary Fund, Exchange Rates selected indicators (Domestic Currency per U.S. dollar, period average). Accessed on May 28, 2022

International Monetary Fund, World Economic Outlook Database (GDP based on Purchasing Power Parity). Accessed on May 28, 2022

National Bureau of Statistics. (2021). Nigeria Poverty Statistics 2021. Retrieved from *https://www.nigerianstat.gov.ng/*

The World Bank. (2021). Nigeria Overview. Retrieved from *https://www.worldbank.org/en/country/nigeria/overview*

United Nations Development Programme. (2020). Human Development Report 2020: The Next Frontier — Human Development and the Anthropocene. New York: United Nations Development Programme.

United Nations. (2021). Sustainable Development Goals. Retrieved from *https://www.un.org/sustainabledevelopment/*

World Economic Forum. (2021). Global Competitiveness Report 2021. Geneva: World Economic Forum.

Transparency International. (2021). Corruption Perceptions Index 2020. Retrieved from https://www.transparency.org/en/cpi/2020/index/nzl

International Monetary Fund. (2021). Nigeria: Staff Concluding Statement of the 2021 Article IV Mission. Retrieved from *https://www.imf.org/en/News/Articles/2021/03/15/pr2161-nigeria-staff-concluding-statement-of-the-2021-article-iv-mission*

Adesina, A. (2019). Africa Can Feed the World, If We Unlock the Potential of Our Young Farmers. World Economic Forum. Retrieved from *https://www.weforum.org/agenda/2019/09/africa-can-feed-the-world-if-we-unlock-the-potential-of-our-young-farmers/*

Ojo, G. (2017). Oil, Conflict, and Poverty: The Nigerian Paradox. Journal of African Conflict and Peace Studies, 1(1), 23-37.

Oyewole, O. (2020). The Future of Nigeria's Infrastructure. McKinsey & Company. Retrieved from *https://www.mckinsey.*

com/industries/capital-projects-and-infrastructure/our-insights/the-future-of-nigerias-infrastructure

World Health Organization. (2021). Nigeria — Health Profile. Retrieved from *https://www.who.int/gho/countries/nga/country_profiles/en/*

International Labour Organization. (2021). Nigeria — Youth Unemployment Rate. Retrieved from *https://www.ilo.org/ilostat-files/Documents/description-EN.pdf*

International Trade Centre, Trade Map. Accessed on May 28, 2022

Investopedia, Net Exports Definition. Accessed on May 28, 2022

Wikipedia, Gross domestic product. Accessed on May 28, 2022

Wikipedia, List of Companies of Nigeria. Accessed on May 28, 2022

Wikipedia, Nigeria. Accessed on May 28, 2022

Wikipedia, Purchasing power parity. Accessed on May 28, 2022

https://www.worldbank.org/en/news/press-release/2021/02/05/nigeria-to-improve-electricity-access-and-services-to-citizens

https://en.wikipedia.org/wiki/Electricity_sector_in_Nigeria

https://www.statista.com/statistics/1278096/solar-energy-capacity-in-nigeria/

https://solarfinanced.africa/solar-projects-in-nigeria-10-largest-solar-power-plants/

https://infoguidenigeria.com/solar-energy-in-nigeria/

https://nigerianprice.com/solar-panel-prices-in-nigeria/

https://www.fao.org/nigeria/fao-in-nigeria/nigeria-at-a-glance/en/

https://www.statista.com/topics/6729/agriculture-in-nigeria/

https://en.wikipedia.org/wiki/Agriculture_in_Nigeria

https://knoema.com/atlas/Nigeria/Food-production-index

https://www.trade.gov/country-commercial-guides/nigeria-agriculture-sector

https://www.bbc.com/news/world-africa-49367968

https://www.trade.gov/country-commercial-guides/nigeria-agriculture-sector

http://wdc.org.ua/en/node/29

https://www.atlanticcouncil.org/blogs/ukrainealert/ukraine-can-feed-the-world/

https://www.agroberichtenbuitenland.nl/actueel/nieuws/2021/07/01/ukraine-land-market

https://www.agroberichtenbuitenland.nl/actueel/nieuws/2021/07/01/ukraine-land-market

https://venturesafrica.com/how-nigeria-can-prevent-its-annual-n3-5-trillion-post-harvest-losses/

https://www.nspri.gov.ng/index.php/en/more/general-news/298-pessu-nigeria-records-50-post-harvest-losses-annually

https://www.blueprint.ng/nigeria-curbing-post-harvest-losses-in-2020/

https://www.forbes.com/sites/zengernews/2023/03/08/tinubus-win-three-things-leaders-should-know-about-nigerias-future/

https://thenewsnigeria.com.ng/2023/03/10/apc-internal-dynam-ics-and-the-future-of-democracy/

https://www.theguardian.com/global-development/2021/oct/25/failed-state-why-nigerias-fragile-democracy-is-facing-an-un-certain-future

https://www.worldbank.org/en/country/nigeria/publication/ni-geria-development-update-ndu

https://businessday.ng/bd-weekender/article/11-nigerian-wom-en-recognized-for-breaking-barriers-empowering-future-leaders/

https://www.tutor2u.net/geography/blog/is-the-future-bright-for-nigeria

https://en.wikipedia.org/wiki/Colonial_Nigeria

https://www.historians.org/teaching-and-learning/teaching-re-sources-for-historians/teaching-and-learning-in-the-digital-age/through-the-lens-of-history-biafra-nigeria-the-west-and-the-world/the-colonial-and-pre-colonial-eras-in-nigeria

https://nigerianscholars.com/tutorials/pre-colonial-politi-cal-systems/pre-colonial-period-in-nigeria/

https://en.wikipedia.org/wiki/Pre-colonial_history_of_Northern_Nigeria

https://en.wikipedia.org/wiki/Colonial_Nigeria

https://en.wikipedia.org/wiki/Colonial_Nigeria

https://www.britannica.com/place/Nigeria/Nigeria-as-a-colony

https://jump.africa/news/how-nigeria-was-colonized-by-the-british-the-complete-history

https://u.osu.edu/introhumanitiesonline/2020/02/04/histo-ry-of-the-british-takeover-of-nigeria/

https://nationaltoday.com/nigeria-independence-day/

https://www.bbc.com/pidgin/58757294

https://www.britannica.com/place/Nigeria/Independent-Nigeria

https://nigerianfinder.com/nigerian-independence-history/

https://bing.com/search?q=the+civil+war+in+nigeria

https://en.wikipedia.org/wiki/Nigerian_Civil_War

https://www.britannica.com/topic/Nigerian-civil-war

https://www.newworldencyclopedia.org/entry/Nigerian_Civil_War

https://bing.com/search?q=the+concept+of+national+-cake+in+nigeria

https://www.researchgate.net/publication/280131102_The_concept_of_national_cake_in_Nigerian_political_system_Implications_for_national_development

https://www.researchgate.net/profile/George-Nche/publication/280131102_The_concept_of_national_cake_in_Nigerian_political_system_Implications_for_national_development/links/55ab78bb08ae815a0427a1a3/The-concept-of-national-cake-in-Nigerian-political-system-Implications-for-national-development.pdf

https://www.academia.edu/41055440/BAKING_THE_NATIONAL_CAKE_IN_CONTEMPORARY_NIGERIA_CHALLENGES_AND_PROSPECTS

https://www.waywordradio.org/national_cake_1/

https://www.transparency.org/en/countries/nigeria

https://www.cfr.org/article/nigerias-all-too-familiar-corruption-ranking-begs-broader-questions-around-normative

https://yasnigeria.org.ng/2021/10/23/corruption-in-nigeria/

https://ganintegrity.com/portal/country-profiles/nigeria/

https://www.unodc.org/nigeria/en/corruption.html

https://en.wikipedia.org/wiki/Corruption_in_Nigeria

https://www.quora.com/How-do-other-African-countries-view-Nigeria

https://en.wikipedia.org/wiki/History_of_Nigeria

https://en.wikipedia.org/wiki/Nigeria

https://guardian.ng/features/what-the-world-can-learn-from-nigeria/

https://www.quora.com/What-can-the-world-learn-from-my-country-Nigeria

https://www.ccn.com/the-socialist-politics-of-envy-what-the-world-can-learn-from-nigerias-unfolding-disaster/

https://www.uzomadozie.com/blog/what-can-nigeria-learn-from-china/

https://bing.com/search?q=current+economic+state+of+affairs+in+nigeria

https://www.usip.org/publications/2021/08/current-situation-nigeria

https://www.worldbank.org/en/country/nigeria/overview

https://www.afdb.org/en/countries-west-africa-nigeria/nigeria-economic-outlook

https://www.worldbank.org/en/country/nigeria/publication/nigeria-economic-update-resilience-through-reforms

https://www.worldstopexports.com/nigerias-top-10-exports/

https://commodity.com/data/nigeria/

https://firstclassnigeria.com/exporting-companies-in-nigeria/

https://lists.ng/top-10-nigerian-exports/

https://en.wikipedia.org/wiki/Mining_industry_of_Nigeria

https://nigerianinfopedia.com/major-mineral-resources-in-nigeria/

https://www.legit.ng/1161400-list-natural-resources-nigeria-locations.html

https://www.oasdom.com/mineral-resources-in-nigeria-and-their-location/

https://healthlink.ng/food-crops-in-nigeria/

https://www.fao.org/nigeria/fao-in-nigeria/nigeria-at-a-glance/en/

https://www.statista.com/statistics/1193512/crop-production-growth-in-nigeria/

https://www.yieldgap.org/Nigeria

https://babbangona.com/agriculture-in-nigeria-7-interesting-facts-statistics/

https://www.msn.com/en-xl/africa/other/pantami-inaugurates-nigeria-startup-act-implementation-committee/ar-AA18royB

https://www.okay.ng/fg-inaugurates-committee-for-implementation-of-nigeria-startup-act-2023/

https://disrupt-africa.com/nigerian-startup-ecosystem-report-2022/

https://samandwright.com/nigerias-tech-startup-ecosystem-and-its-pertinent-challenges/

https://www.cia.gov/the-world-factbook/countries/nigeria/

https://www.bbc.com/news/world-africa-47217557

https://www.nairaland.com/864287/what-does-nigeria-contribute-world

https://www.internetgeography.net/topics/what-is-nigerias-location-and-importance/